California
COMMON CORE
SBAC

Grade 8 English Language Arts/Literacy

SUCCESS STRATEGIES

Common Core Test Review for the
California Smarter
Balanced Assessments,
Part of the California Assessment of Student
Performance and Progress (CAASPP) System

Dear Future Exam Success Story:

First of all, **THANK YOU** for purchasing Mometrix study materials!

Second, congratulations! You are one of the few determined test-takers who are committed to doing whatever it takes to excel on your exam. **You have come to the right place.** We developed these study materials with one goal in mind: to deliver you the information you need in a format that's concise and easy to use.

In addition to optimizing your guide for the content of the test, we've outlined our recommended steps for breaking down the preparation process into small, attainable goals so you can make sure you stay on track.

We've also analyzed the entire test-taking process, identifying the most common pitfalls and showing how you can overcome them and be ready for any curveball the test throws you.

Standardized testing is one of the biggest obstacles on your road to success, which only increases the importance of doing well in the high-pressure, high-stakes environment of test day. Your results on this test could have a significant impact on your future, and this guide provides the information and practical advice to help you achieve your full potential on test day.

Your success is our success

We would love to hear from you! If you would like to share the story of your exam success or if you have any questions or comments in regard to our products, please contact us at **800-673-8175** or **support@mometrix.com**.

Thanks again for your business and we wish you continued success!

Sincerely,
The Mometrix Test Preparation Team

Need more help? Check out our flashcards at:
http://MometrixFlashcards.com/CaliforniaStandardsTests

Copyright © 2020 by Mometrix Media LLC. All rights reserved.
Written and edited by the Mometrix Test Preparation Team
Printed in the United States of America

TABLE OF CONTENTS

INTRODUCTION 1

SUCCESS STRATEGY #1 – PLAN BIG, STUDY SMALL 2
- INFORMATION ORGANIZATION 2
- TIME MANAGEMENT 2
- STUDY ENVIRONMENT 2

SUCCESS STRATEGY #2 – MAKE YOUR STUDYING COUNT 3
- RETENTION 3
- MODALITY 3

SUCCESS STRATEGY #3 – PRACTICE THE RIGHT WAY 4
- PRACTICE TEST STRATEGY 5

SUCCESS STRATEGY #4 – PACE YOURSELF 6

TEST-TAKING STRATEGIES 7
- QUESTION STRATEGIES 7
- ANSWER CHOICE STRATEGIES 8
- GENERAL STRATEGIES 9
- FINAL NOTES 10

READING 12
- LITERATURE 12
- INFORMATIONAL TEXTS 18

WRITING 26
- PERSUASIVE TEXT 28
- INFORMATIONAL OR EXPLANATORY TEXT 30
- NARRATIVES 32

SPEAKING AND LISTENING 36
- DISCUSSIONS 36
- PRESENTATIONS 37

LANGUAGE 39

ENGLISH LANGUAGE ARTS/LITERACY PRACTICE TEST #1 45
- PRACTICE QUESTIONS 45
- ANSWERS AND EXPLANATIONS 57

ENGLISH LANGUAGE ARTS/LITERACY PRACTICE TEST #2 60
- PRACTICE QUESTIONS 60
- ANSWERS AND EXPLANATIONS 71

HOW TO OVERCOME TEST ANXIETY 74
- CAUSES OF TEST ANXIETY 74
- ELEMENTS OF TEST ANXIETY 75
- EFFECTS OF TEST ANXIETY 75
- PHYSICAL STEPS FOR BEATING TEST ANXIETY 76
- MENTAL STEPS FOR BEATING TEST ANXIETY 77
- STUDY STRATEGY 78
- TEST TIPS 80
- IMPORTANT QUALIFICATION 81

THANK YOU	82
ADDITIONAL BONUS MATERIAL	83

Introduction

Thank you for purchasing this resource! You have made the choice to prepare yourself for a test that could have a huge impact on your future, and this guide is designed to help you be fully ready for test day. Obviously, it's important to have a solid understanding of the test material, but you also need to be prepared for the unique environment and stressors of the test, so that you can perform to the best of your abilities.

For this purpose, the first section that appears in this guide is the **Success Strategies**. We've devoted countless hours to meticulously researching what works and what doesn't, and we've boiled down our findings to the five most impactful steps you can take to improve your performance on the test. We start at the beginning with study planning and move through the preparation process, all the way to the testing strategies that will help you get the most out of what you know when you're finally sitting in front of the test.

We recommend that you start preparing for your test as far in advance as possible. However, if you've bought this guide as a last-minute study resource and only have a few days before your test, we recommend that you skip over the first two Success Strategies since they address a long-term study plan.

If you struggle with **test anxiety**, we strongly encourage you to check out our recommendations for how you can overcome it. Test anxiety is a formidable foe, but it can be beaten, and we want to make sure you have the tools you need to defeat it.

Success Strategy #1 – Plan Big, Study Small

There's a lot riding on your performance. If you want to ace this test, you're going to need to keep your skills sharp and the material fresh in your mind. You need a plan that lets you review everything you need to know while still fitting in your schedule. We'll break this strategy down into three categories.

Information Organization

Start with the information you already have: the official test outline. From this, you can make a complete list of all the concepts you need to cover before the test. Organize these concepts into groups that can be studied together, and create a list of any related vocabulary you need to learn so you can brush up on any difficult terms. You'll want to keep this vocabulary list handy once you actually start studying since you may need to add to it along the way.

Time Management

Once you have your set of study concepts, decide how to spread them out over the time you have left before the test. Break your study plan into small, clear goals so you have a manageable task for each day and know exactly what you're doing. Then just focus on one small step at a time. When you manage your time this way, you don't need to spend hours at a time studying. Studying a small block of content for a short period each day helps you retain information better and avoid stressing over how much you have left to do. You can relax knowing that you have a plan to cover everything in time. In order for this strategy to be effective though, you have to start studying early and stick to your schedule. Avoid the exhaustion and futility that comes from last-minute cramming!

Study Environment

The environment you study in has a big impact on your learning. Studying in a coffee shop, while probably more enjoyable, is not likely to be as fruitful as studying in a quiet room. It's important to keep distractions to a minimum. You're only planning to study for a short block of time, so make the most of it. Don't pause to check your phone or get up to find a snack. It's also important to **avoid multitasking**. Research has consistently shown that multitasking will make your studying dramatically less effective. Your study area should also be comfortable and well-lit so you don't have the distraction of straining your eyes or sitting on an uncomfortable chair.

The time of day you study is also important. You want to be rested and alert. Don't wait until just before bedtime. Study when you'll be most likely to comprehend and remember. Even better, if you know what time of day your test will be, set that time aside for study. That way your brain will be used to working on that subject at that specific time and you'll have a better chance of recalling information.

Finally, it can be helpful to team up with others who are studying for the same test. Your actual studying should be done in as isolated an environment as possible, but the work of organizing the information and setting up the study plan can be divided up. In between study sessions, you can discuss with your teammates the concepts that you're all studying and quiz each other on the details. Just be sure that your teammates are as serious about the test as you are. If you find that your study time is being replaced with social time, you might need to find a new team.

Success Strategy #2 – Make Your Studying Count

You're devoting a lot of time and effort to preparing for this test, so you want to be absolutely certain it will pay off. This means doing more than just reading the content and hoping you can remember it on test day. It's important to make every minute of study count. There are two main areas you can focus on to make your studying count:

Retention

It doesn't matter how much time you study if you can't remember the material. You need to make sure you are retaining the concepts. To check your retention of the information you're learning, try recalling it at later times with minimal prompting. Try carrying around flashcards and glance at one or two from time to time or ask a friend who's also studying for the test to quiz you.

To enhance your retention, look for ways to put the information into practice so that you can apply it rather than simply recalling it. If you're using the information in practical ways, it will be much easier to remember. Similarly, it helps to solidify a concept in your mind if you're not only reading it to yourself but also explaining it to someone else. Ask a friend to let you teach them about a concept you're a little shaky on (or speak aloud to an imaginary audience if necessary). As you try to summarize, define, give examples, and answer your friend's questions, you'll understand the concepts better and they will stay with you longer. Finally, step back for a big picture view and ask yourself how each piece of information fits with the whole subject. When you link the different concepts together and see them working together as a whole, it's easier to remember the individual components.

Finally, practice showing your work on any multi-step problems, even if you're just studying. Writing out each step you take to solve a problem will help solidify the process in your mind, and you'll be more likely to remember it during the test.

Modality

Modality simply refers to the means or method by which you study. Choosing a study modality that fits your own individual learning style is crucial. No two people learn best in exactly the same way, so it's important to know your strengths and use them to your advantage.

For example, if you learn best by visualization, focus on visualizing a concept in your mind and draw an image or a diagram. Try color-coding your notes, illustrating them, or creating symbols that will trigger your mind to recall a learned concept. If you learn best by hearing or discussing information, find a study partner who learns the same way or read aloud to yourself. Think about how to put the information in your own words. Imagine that you are giving a lecture on the topic and record yourself so you can listen to it later.

For any learning style, flashcards can be helpful. Organize the information so you can take advantage of spare moments to review. Underline key words or phrases. Use different colors for different categories. Mnemonic devices (such as creating a short list in which every item starts with the same letter) can also help with retention. Find what works best for you and use it to store the information in your mind most effectively and easily.

Success Strategy #3 – Practice the Right Way

Your success on test day depends not only on how many hours you put into preparing, but also on whether you prepared the right way. It's good to check along the way to see if your studying is paying off. One of the most effective ways to do this is by taking practice tests to evaluate your progress. Practice tests are useful because they show exactly where you need to improve. Every time you take a practice test, pay special attention to these three groups of questions:

- The questions you got wrong
- The questions you had to guess on, even if you guessed right
- The questions you found difficult or slow to work through

This will show you exactly what your weak areas are, and where you need to devote more study time. Ask yourself why each of these questions gave you trouble. Was it because you didn't understand the material? Was it because you didn't remember the vocabulary? Do you need more repetitions on this type of question to build speed and confidence? Dig into those questions and figure out how you can strengthen your weak areas as you go back to review the material.

Additionally, many practice tests have a section explaining the answer choices. It can be tempting to read the explanation and think that you now have a good understanding of the concept. However, an explanation likely only covers part of the question's broader context. Even if the explanation makes sense, **go back and investigate** every concept related to the question until you're positive you have a thorough understanding.

As you go along, keep in mind that the practice test is just that: practice. Memorizing these questions and answers will not be very helpful on the actual test because it is unlikely to have any of the same exact questions. If you only know the right answers to the sample questions, you won't be prepared for the real thing. **Study the concepts** until you understand them fully, and then you'll be able to answer any question that shows up on the test.

It's important to wait on the practice tests until you're ready. If you take a test on your first day of study, you may be overwhelmed by the amount of material covered and how much you need to learn. Work up to it gradually.

On test day, you'll need to be prepared for answering questions, managing your time, and using the test-taking strategies you've learned. It's a lot to balance, like a mental marathon that will have a big impact on your future. Like training for a marathon, you'll need to start slowly and work your way up. When test day arrives, you'll be ready.

Start with what you've read in the first two Success Strategies—plan your course and study in the way that works best for you. If you have time, consider using multiple study resources to get different approaches to the same concepts. It can be helpful to see difficult concepts from more than one angle. Then find a good source for practice tests. Many times, the test website will suggest potential study resources or provide sample tests.

Practice Test Strategy

If you're able to find at least three practice tests, we recommend this strategy:

Untimed and Open-Book Practice

Take the first test with no time constraints and with your notes and study guide handy. Take your time and focus on applying the strategies you've learned.

Timed and Open-Book Practice

Take the second practice test open-book as well, but set a timer and practice pacing yourself to finish in time.

Timed and Closed-Book Practice

Take any other practice tests as if it were test day. Set a timer and put away your study materials. Sit at a table or desk in a quiet room, imagine yourself at the testing center, and answer questions as quickly and accurately as possible.

Keep repeating timed and closed-book tests on a regular basis until you run out of practice tests or it's time for the actual test. Your mind will be ready for the schedule and stress of test day, and you'll be able to focus on recalling the material you've learned.

Success Strategy #4 – Pace Yourself

Once you're fully prepared for the material on the test, your biggest challenge on test day will be managing your time. Just knowing that the clock is ticking can make you panic even if you have plenty of time left. Work on pacing yourself so you can build confidence against the time constraints of the exam. Pacing is a difficult skill to master, especially in a high-pressure environment, so **practice is vital**.

Set time expectations for your pace based on how much time is available. For example, if a section has 60 questions and the time limit is 30 minutes, you know you have to average 30 seconds or less per question in order to answer them all. Although 30 seconds is the hard limit, set 25 seconds per question as your goal, so you reserve extra time to spend on harder questions. When you budget extra time for the harder questions, you no longer have any reason to stress when those questions take longer to answer.

Don't let this time expectation distract you from working through the test at a calm, steady pace, but keep it in mind so you don't spend too much time on any one question. Recognize that taking extra time on one question you don't understand may keep you from answering two that you do understand later in the test. If your time limit for a question is up and you're still not sure of the answer, mark it and move on, and come back to it later if the time and the test format allow. If the testing format doesn't allow you to return to earlier questions, just make an educated guess; then put it out of your mind and move on.

On the easier questions, be careful not to rush. It may seem wise to hurry through them so you have more time for the challenging ones, but it's not worth missing one if you know the concept and just didn't take the time to read the question fully. Work efficiently but make sure you understand the question and have looked at all of the answer choices, since more than one may seem right at first.

Even if you're paying attention to the time, you may find yourself a little behind at some point. You should speed up to get back on track, but do so wisely. Don't panic; just take a few seconds less on each question until you're caught up. Don't guess without thinking, but do look through the answer choices and eliminate any you know are wrong. If you can get down to two choices, it is often worthwhile to guess from those. Once you've chosen an answer, move on and don't dwell on any that you skipped or had to hurry through. If a question was taking too long, chances are it was one of the harder ones, so you weren't as likely to get it right anyway.

On the other hand, if you find yourself getting ahead of schedule, it may be beneficial to slow down a little. The more quickly you work, the more likely you are to make a careless mistake that will affect your score. You've budgeted time for each question, so don't be afraid to spend that time. Practice an efficient but careful pace to get the most out of the time you have.

Test-Taking Strategies

This section contains a list of test-taking strategies that you may find helpful as you work through the test. By taking what you know and applying logical thought, you can maximize your chances of answering any question correctly!

It is very important to realize that every question is different and every person is different: no single strategy will work on every question, and no single strategy will work for every person. That's why we've included all of them here, so you can try them out and determine which ones work best for different types of questions and which ones work best for you.

Question Strategies

Read Carefully

Read the question and answer choices carefully. Don't miss the question because you misread the terms. You have plenty of time to read each question thoroughly and make sure you understand what is being asked. Yet a happy medium must be attained, so don't waste too much time. You must read carefully, but efficiently.

Contextual Clues

Look for contextual clues. If the question includes a word you are not familiar with, look at the immediate context for some indication of what the word might mean. Contextual clues can often give you all the information you need to decipher the meaning of an unfamiliar word. Even if you can't determine the meaning, you may be able to narrow down the possibilities enough to make a solid guess at the answer to the question.

Prefixes

If you're having trouble with a word in the question or answer choices, try dissecting it. Take advantage of every clue that the word might include. Prefixes and suffixes can be a huge help. Usually they allow you to determine a basic meaning. Pre- means before, post- means after, pro - is positive, de- is negative. From prefixes and suffixes, you can get an idea of the general meaning of the word and try to put it into context.

Hedge Words

Watch out for critical hedge words, such as *likely, may, can, sometimes, often, almost, mostly, usually, generally, rarely,* and *sometimes*. Question writers insert these hedge phrases to cover every possibility. Often an answer choice will be wrong simply because it leaves no room for exception. Be on guard for answer choices that have definitive words such as *exactly* and *always*.

Switchback Words

Stay alert for *switchbacks*. These are the words and phrases frequently used to alert you to shifts in thought. The most common switchback words are *but, although,* and *however*. Others include *nevertheless, on the other hand, even though, while, in spite of, despite, regardless of*. Switchback words are important to catch because they can change the direction of the question or an answer choice.

Face Value

When in doubt, use common sense. Accept the situation in the problem at face value. Don't read too much into it. These problems will not require you to make wild assumptions. If you have to go beyond creativity and warp time or space in order to have an answer choice fit the question, then you should move on and consider the other answer choices. These are normal problems rooted in reality. The applicable relationship or explanation may not be readily apparent, but it is there for you to figure out. Use your common sense to interpret anything that isn't clear.

Answer Choice Strategies

Answer Selection

The most thorough way to pick an answer choice is to identify and eliminate wrong answers until only one is left, then confirm it is the correct answer. Sometimes an answer choice may immediately seem right, but be careful. The test writers will usually put more than one reasonable answer choice on each question, so take a second to read all of them and make sure that the other choices are not equally obvious. As long as you have time left, it is better to read every answer choice than to pick the first one that looks right without checking the others.

Answer Choice Families

An answer choice family consists of two (in rare cases, three) answer choices that are very similar in construction and cannot all be true at the same time. If you see two answer choices that are direct opposites or parallels, one of them is usually the correct answer. For instance, if one answer choice says that quantity x increases and another either says that quantity x decreases (opposite) or says that quantity y increases (parallel), then those answer choices would fall into the same family. An answer choice that doesn't match the construction of the answer choice family is more likely to be incorrect. Most questions will not have answer choice families, but when they do appear, you should be prepared to recognize them.

Eliminate Answers

Eliminate answer choices as soon as you realize they are wrong, but make sure you consider all possibilities. If you are eliminating answer choices and realize that the last one you are left with is also wrong, don't panic. Start over and consider each choice again. There may be something you missed the first time that you will realize on the second pass.

Avoid Fact Traps

Don't be distracted by an answer choice that is factually true but doesn't answer the question. You are looking for the choice that answers the question. Stay focused on what the question is asking for so you don't accidentally pick an answer that is true but incorrect. Always go back to the question and make sure the answer choice you've selected actually answers the question and is not merely a true statement.

Extreme Statements

In general, you should avoid answers that put forth extreme actions as standard practice or proclaim controversial ideas as established fact. An answer choice that states the "process should be used in certain situations, if…" is much more likely to be correct than one that states the "process should be discontinued completely." The first is a calm rational statement and doesn't even make a definitive, uncompromising stance, using a hedge word *if* to provide wiggle room, whereas the second choice is a radical idea and far more extreme.

Benchmark

As you read through the answer choices and you come across one that seems to answer the question well, mentally select that answer choice. This is not your final answer, but it's the one that will help you evaluate the other answer choices. The one that you selected is your benchmark or standard for judging each of the other answer choices. Every other answer choice must be compared to your benchmark. That choice is correct until proven otherwise by another answer choice beating it. If you find a better answer, then that one becomes your new benchmark. Once you've decided that no other choice answers the question as well as your benchmark, you have your final answer.

Predict the Answer

Before you even start looking at the answer choices, it is often best to try to predict the answer. When you come up with the answer on your own, it is easier to avoid distractions and traps because you will know exactly what to look for. The right answer choice is unlikely to be word-for-word what you came up with, but it should be a close match. Even if you are confident that you have the right answer, you should still take the time to read each option before moving on.

General Strategies

Tough Questions

If you are stumped on a problem or it appears too hard or too difficult, don't waste time. Move on! Remember though, if you can quickly check for obviously incorrect answer choices, your chances of guessing correctly are greatly improved. Before you completely give up, at least try to knock out a couple of possible answers. Eliminate what you can and then guess at the remaining answer choices before moving on.

Check Your Work

Since you will probably not know every term listed and the answer to every question, it is important that you get credit for the ones that you do know. Don't miss any questions through careless mistakes. If at all possible, try to take a second to look back over your answer selection and make sure you've selected the correct answer choice and haven't made a costly careless mistake (such as marking an answer choice that you didn't mean to mark). This quick double check should more than pay for itself in caught mistakes for the time it costs.

Pace Yourself

It's easy to be overwhelmed when you're looking at a page full of questions; your mind is confused and full of random thoughts, and the clock is ticking down faster than you would like. Calm down and maintain the pace that you have set for yourself. Especially as you get down to the last few minutes of the test, don't let the small numbers on the clock make you panic. As long as you are on track by monitoring your pace, you are guaranteed to have time for each question.

Don't Rush

It is very easy to make errors when you are in a hurry. Maintaining a fast pace in answering questions is pointless if it makes you miss questions that you would have gotten right otherwise. Test writers like to include distracting information and wrong answers that seem right. Taking a little extra time to avoid careless mistakes can make all the difference in your test score. Find a pace that allows you to be confident in the answers that you select.

Keep Moving

Panicking will not help you pass the test, so do your best to stay calm and keep moving. Taking deep breaths and going through the answer elimination steps you practiced can help to break through a stress barrier and keep your pace.

Final Notes

The combination of a solid foundation of content knowledge and the confidence that comes from practicing your plan for applying that knowledge is the key to maximizing your performance on test day. As your foundation of content knowledge is built up and strengthened, you'll find that the strategies included in this chapter become more and more effective in helping you quickly sift through the distractions and traps of the test to isolate the correct answer.

Now it's time to move on to the test content chapters of this book, but be sure to keep your goal in mind. As you read, think about how you will be able to apply this information on the test. If you've already seen sample questions for the test and you have an idea of the question format and style, try to come up with questions of your own that you can answer based on what you're reading. This will give you valuable practice applying your knowledge in the same ways you can expect to on test day.

Good luck and good studying!

Reading

Literature

Explicit information

Explicit information is the information that is found in a passage or story. This information can include facts, descriptions, and statements about the characters, setting, or events in a story. Explicit information is not suggested or hinted at; it is definite because it is stated right in the passage. Explicit information takes many shapes; in a description it might be that "Tom was taller than his brother." In dialogue it could be, "I have never been to Texas before." Or it could be found in an event: "Charles hit his head on the bottom of the swimming pool." Explicit information is often used as supporting evidence when making an inference.

Identify the explicit information in the following excerpt.

> Bernard loved to paint. He regularly worked eight hours a day, six days a week, perfecting his craft. His sister Julie was an actress. On days when she was performing or rehearsing, she put in very long hours. Sometimes she worked 14 or 16 hours a day.

Explicit information is information which is found within the text itself. It is not suggested in any way. This excerpt tells about a brother and sister and what they did. It tells us that Bernard loved to paint and worked on his painting eight hours a day. It also says that his sister Julie was an actress and that he sometimes rehearsed 14 or 16 hours a day. This information is all explicit. It is stated in the excerpt. The reader does not need to make an inference or guess at anything. Everything is factual. When you read, think about the information in the story and whether it is explicit or not.

Inference

An *inference* is basically a good guess that a reader makes using the explicit information that is in a passage or story. An inference can also be based on personal experience combined with the information in a passage. For instance, a story may say that several people are leaving a movie theater and many of them are crying. The logical conclusion, both from the explicit information and personal knowledge, is that the movie was sad. A good inference is supported by the information in a passage. Inferences are different from explicit information: they are not clearly stated in a passage, only hinted at. The reader must determine—or *infer*—for himself what the author is suggesting. A good reader puts the clues together to produce a conclusion that is both logical and likely to be true.

Read the following excerpt and decide why Alex did not want to see the puppy.

> Dr. Thomas walked up to Alex in the waiting room. He spoke as gently as he could. "I'm sorry about Rover. We did everything we could to save him. But he was just too sick. I know how much you loved him. But I have something to show you." Then Dr. Thomas showed Alex a cute little puppy. "No," the boy shouted. "I don't want to see your dog."

You can infer that Alex did not want to see the puppy because he was too upset about his own dog. This conclusion might be based both on what the passage says and from personal experience. In the excerpt, Dr. Thomas tells Alex that they could not save his dog. From personal experience you might realize how upsetting it is to lose a pet. That would help you come to the conclusion that Alex was grieving and didn't want to see another dog at that moment. An inference is based on the information in a passage and a reader's experience, but it is not stated in the text.

Determining the theme of a story

The *theme* of a story is the lesson that it teaches. It is what the reader learns from what happens in a story. The theme is linked to the characters, the setting, and the events in a story. The theme develops with the development of the plot. Some themes are fairly common. These themes are called *universal themes*; they suggest things about life, society, and human nature. Themes are an important part of literature because they serve the purpose of teaching the reader or listener a truth about life. The theme is developed by how a character or characters respond to their situations and challenges.

Tell why the theme of the following excerpt should be "Overconfidence can lead to a fall."
> Bella was happy. She auditioned for the starring role in the school play and she felt sure she'd got the part. Afterwards, she told her friends she would be starring in the play. But on Tuesday when the director said they had offered the part to Sara Goodwin, she started crying.

The excerpt tells the story of a girl who has an audition and thinks she got the starring role. She is so confident that she even tells her friends that she has the part. But then she learns that the role was offered to someone else and she starts to cry. She was overly confident about her success and was subsequently devastated when she learned of her failure, and that is the lesson of the story. If you are overly confident you may have a fall. That is the theme of the story. A theme is the lesson that a story teaches. This particular theme is found often in literature. A theme is not stated in a passage: the reader must deduce it from the plot of the story.

Objective summary

An *objective summary* of a story has several components. It should include the main idea of the story, the most important details or events that occur, and the main characters and what happens to them. A summary is not a general statement about what a story is about, nor is it a paraphrase. Paraphrases retell a story and give too much information about what happens, including some that is not important; summaries do not. A summary will not include everything in the story. In order to write an objective summary, you will need to think about what happens in the story. You will need to decide what it is mostly about and what details are the most important. Objective summaries do not include personal feelings or opinions.

Read the summary and discuss how it could be improved.
> This story is about a man and a woman who moved to the West many years ago. There was a lot of information about covered wagons or "prairie schooners," as they called them. I liked the story because of that.

The summary tells the main idea of the story, but it doesn't include the details of what happens in the story. It does not include the main characters and what they did or what challenges they faced. It does not summarize the plot. Another problem with the summary is that it is not objective; it is subjective. The writer describes what he thinks about the story. But personal opinions have no place in an objective summary of a story. To improve it, the writer should remove his personal opinion and add descriptions of who was in the story, what important things happened to them, and how the story ended.

Driving the action

There are many ways in which the action of a story may be driven. Dialogue is one of them. What a character says either to another character or about a situation may propel the action by revealing what a character is thinking or what he may do. Similarly, what a character says will tell the audience what he is like. His manner of speaking, what he says, and how he says it are all clues to his personality. Dialogue can also provoke a decision by showing what the character intends to do in the future. Incidents in a story also propel the action because the plot is made up of events that build on events. Incidents such as a confrontation could reveal aspects of a character or provoke a decision.

Read the excerpt and tell how it reveals aspects of the speaker.
> I told you I wasn't ever going to become a doctor and yet here you are bringing the topic up again. I think I am just going to put a sign on my door that says "No Medical School." Are you going to harangue me all day?

The person who is speaking sounds very sure of what he does not want to do and is forcefully resisting any attempt by someone else, a person not revealed, to try to get him to go to medical school. The speaker's character is resolute and somewhat dramatic because he plans to put a sign on his door to remind the unnamed person that he has no intention of doing what the other person wants. It could be a parent, a wife or even a friend who is urging this action. The character also seems somewhat young because he seems to have to defend his decision so strongly.

Read the excerpt and tell how this incident propels the action of the story and provokes a decision.
> It was a perfect day it seemed, until Sam saw the thunderheads roll in. He knew that it would be dangerous to be in a rowboat in the middle of the lake during a thunder and lightning storm. Suddenly the sky became darker and he heard a clap of thunder.

This incident certainly propels the action of the story. It would appear that Sam is in a rowboat in the middle of the lake having a lovely time when he hears a clap of thunder. He realizes that a lake is a dangerous place to be so this event means that Sam must take action. What that action is would be of interest to the reader because it will help form the plot of the story. The incident also forces Sam to make a decision about what he should do. This will help the reader better understand Sam as a character.

Context clues

Context clues are one of the best tools in understanding the meaning of unknown words or phrases. The sentence that contains the word or phrase and the sentences before and after the unknown word or phrase often have clues that suggest the meaning. When attempting to understand what a word or phrase means, try to think of a synonym and then replace the unknown word with the synonym to see if it makes sense in the sentence. Many words have more than one meaning, so it is only the context that will tell the reader what is meant. For instance, the word "bluff" can mean a trick or a kind of hill. In the sentence "He stood on a bluff overlooking the ocean," the context is clear. In this instance it means a type of hill.

Read the following sentences and tell how to understand the meaning of "sedentary."

> I like my job typing medical records except for one thing. I find it very sedentary. I would rather have a job where I can move around more.

"Sedentary" means "inactive" or "deskbound." When you read the excerpt you can determine the meaning from the context clues. The selection tells you that the author likes his job except for one thing and that he would rather have a job that allowed him to move around more. This clue helps you understand what "sedentary" means. If you insert the synonyms "inactive" or "deskbound" in place of "sedentary," you can see that the excerpt makes sense. Context clues help you understand the meanings of unknown words. Context clues are hints as to the meaning of a word or phrase.

Figurative language

Figurative language is the use of words and expressions to expand reality in a vivid way. It is the use of language in a non-literal way, which means using language in a non-traditional manner in order to create an image. It is often used by poets. Examples of figurative language include simile, metaphor, personification, hyperbole, onomatopoeia and alliteration. *Similes* compare things using the words "like" or "as," for example, "She is as gentle as a lamb." *Metaphors* compare things without using comparing words: "She is a lamb when dealing with others." *Personification* gives a thing or animal human traits: "The ocean spoke of foreign places and dreams." *Hyperbole* is an exaggeration that is vivid but not believable: "She is the kindest person in the world." *Onomatopoeia* is when words sound like what they are, such as "hiss, hiss" to describe the sound a snake makes. *Alliteration* is the use of consecutive words that start with the same letter: "Raining, ripping, racing, running…"

Read the excerpt and tell what form of figurative language the phrase "come down like a sluggish sea" is and why.

> The weather changed. The air had come down like a sluggish sea, weighing us down with its heavy pressure.

The phrase, "air had come down like a sluggish sea" is an example of a simile. Similes add depth to writing and make it richer. They are used to create a more vivid image of something in the reader's mind. In this case, the air coming down "like a sluggish sea" means the air is very heavy. The phrase is not a metaphor because it compares to things using a comparison word, in this case "like." It can't be hyperbole as there is no exaggeration in the phrase. It is not an example of personification or onomatopoeia either, although there is a hint of alliteration in the phrase.

Denotative vs. connotative meaning of words

Words often have both a denotative meaning and a connotative meaning. The *denotative meaning* is the dictionary definition of a word. The *connotative meaning* is the associations that a word carries with it, associations above and beyond its literal meaning. For instance, the word "decorative" is a synonym for "fancy," but so is the word "extravagant." Yet "extravagant" has a rather negative meaning where "decorative" does not. "Extravagant" suggests something that is overdone or excessive. Readers should recognize the connotative meanings that writers include in their stories in order to better understand the writers' intent.

Read the following sentence and explain the connotative meanings of "strong-willed" and how it compares to "pig-headed."

> Some people admired Uncle Fred because they thought he was strong-willed, but others considered him pig-headed.

Both the words "strong-willed" and "pig-headed" have the literal or denotative meaning of "stubborn." The word "pig-headed," however, also has a rather negative connotation of being so stubborn to the point of being stupid and that people are frustrated by such a person, while "strong-willed" has a more positive meaning of being stubborn as a good characteristic. The connotations that a word add to a sentence will influence how the reader interprets a story's characters and events. That is why it is important to notice which words the writer chooses to use. In this instance, the writer has drawn a contrast between positive and negative.

Read the excerpt and tell how the analogy impacts the tone of the story.

> Clara nestled underneath a tree, with her book, much in the same way that Alice of Wonderland fame might have done. Then, just like Alice, she fell asleep.

The words that a writer uses to tell a story are important because they can evoke a strong reaction in a reader. Here the writer makes an analogy to "Alice in Wonderland" in the way he describes Clara nestled under a tree with a book. The story of "Alice in Wonderland" is well known, and by making a reference to it, the writer creates a mood of mystery and tension about what may happen. The reader finds himself wondering if Clara will encounter some of the characters that Alice did when she says that Clara fell asleep. When reading, make sure to be aware of any analogy or references that the author makes to other texts to better comprehend what the author is suggesting.

Comparing and contrasting the structure of a poem to a short story

Poems have many structures. There are sonnets, haiku, and even pattern poems that take the shape of the focus of the poem. Poetry has developed over many years and its structure can be strict or, in the case of free verse, without rules. Generally a sonnet is a 14-line structure with a specific rhyming pattern and meter. Sonnets have been popular for a very long time and were a specialty of William Shakespeare. Haiku is a Japanese form of poetry that features three lines of five, seven, and five syllables, respectively. There are no strictures that are similar in a short story. Stories follow the order of the plot: the beginning, middle and end. But even that is not always the case with modern fiction, which may lack a real beginning or a definite end. Again the structure plays into the meaning and style of the poem or story by signaling to the reader the intent.

Dramatic irony

Dramatic irony is a situation when a character makes a remark about doing something that seems harmless in its context, but that the audience has more information about and realizes it could result in something unpleasant. This difference in knowledge can create suspense or humor depending on the circumstances. For instance, if a character says, "I will have a cup of tea now," and the audience knows that there is poison in the tea, it creates a situation that is suspenseful. That is an example of dramatic irony. The word "irony" comes from the Greek word for "dissembling" and it was used to describe what the Greeks thought was the gap between appearance and reality.

Transforming a story to a live performance

When transforming a story or drama to a live performance, either on stage or in film, a director will need to make decisions on how to present the story. Certainly the experience of seeing a performance of a story or drama is different because actors are speaking the dialogue or lines and are bringing the words and characters to life. But many directors choose to change the dialogue to simplify or emphasize a certain aspect of the play or film. Another decision that might be made in a staged performance is how the characters act; they may do something differently from what a person might imagine when reading a script. Yet another factor that might be different is the time period in which the action takes place. In particular, in both filmed and staged versions of Shakespearean plays, directors sometimes choose to bring the action into a modern world rather than keep it set in the time of the Renaissance.

How a filmed production of the story of Snow White might be different from the written story

In a filmed production of Snow White, you would see Snow White as a person who has certain traits that might be different from the written character. Also the evil stepmother might be better rendered and the reasons that she hated Snow White might be made clearer. Some directors might make the evil queen justified in her hatred of Snow White. For instance, a television series called "Once Upon a Time" presents these fairy tale characters in ways very different from the popular perception of them, giving reasons for their actions that were not included in the famous story.

How a modern fiction draws from the past

There is an old saying that writers like to quote: "there's nothing new under the sun." And to a large extent this is true because many of the modern stories, themes, patterns of events, and character types are taken from traditional stories, myths or religious works and then changed to make them seem new. For instance, the film "Wrath of the Titans," which is a sequel takes up where its predecessor, "Clash of the Titans," ended. These films are based on the myth of the ancient Greek hero Perseus and the tale of his life, which most people do not know. But that fact is unimportant because the movie makes the plot readily available to them. Mainstream actors give these mythic characters life, and the movies are filled with action to excite the audience by bringing an ancient tale to life while using the most advanced technology to create special effects. While the story is from myth, the director makes it current in that the actors bring color and personality to the mythic people they play.

Importance of being able to read and comprehend a wide variety of texts by the end of grade 8

It is vital that, by the time a student completes grade 8, he or she will be able to read and comprehend literature, including stories, dramas, and poetry, at the grade 8 level. Students need that level of comprehension in order to have a basis for furthering their ability to read and experience the many great classics of literature that are at that level. It will also build a foundation for the student to read even more difficult texts as he or she enters high school. The ability to read and comprehend literature will lead to a student having a sound background in the cultural aspect of literature and will give the student an excellent background and preparation for whatever the student wishes to pursue in his or her life. It is also an excellent aid to learning more vocabulary.

Informational Texts

Finding textual evidence

Explicit information is information that is stated in a text. It is not something that is hinted at. A nonfiction text is usually made up of a main idea and supporting details. These supporting details are explicit: they are stated right in the text. They can be used to support an inference that is not stated in the text, or to support the main claims of an essay. Supporting information should be based on fact, not opinion. It should come from a reliable source and be something that others can verify. When trying to find textual evidence for what a text says explicitly, you will need to look for details that give more information about it.

Read the following excerpt and identify which information is explicit.

> In ancient times the value of an ox was the basis for the monetary systems of the Greeks, Assyrians, Mesopotamians, and the Egyptians. Each of these territories had their own currency. For instance, Egypt traded in gold and Greece in silver or copper.

All of the information in the excerpt is explicit. Nothing is hinted at. It says that the value of an ox was the basis for the monetary system for ancient Greeks, Assyrians, Mesopotamians, and the Egyptians. It adds that each of these territories had their own currency. It further informs that Egypt traded in gold and Greece in silver or copper. All of this information is factual. There are no opinions in the excerpt. There is nothing with which to make an inference. The details support the main idea that the ancients had monetary systems. All of the information can be checked to see if it is accurate.

Inference

An inference is a best guess. It is a conclusion that a reader can make from the information in a passage. For instance, if a passage says that a man is running down the street holding a woman's handbag, and there is a woman yelling for help in the distance, someone watching the scene might come up with the conclusion that the man is a thief and has stolen the woman's handbag. It could be an incorrect conclusion, but based on the evidence in the passage, it is the best guess that can be made. When you make an inference, you need to be able to tell what textual evidence supports the conclusion or inference. In this case, the fact that a man is running away holding a woman's handbag and a woman is yelling for help leads you to the conclusion.

Identify which information in the excerpt supports the inference that plants need more water when it is hot than when it is cool.

Sweat is water that evaporates on the skin. Sweating is a process which cools the body. People sweat more in hot weather. Similarly, plants are cooled by evaporating water. Most of the water a plant takes in is used to keep it cool.

The information that supports the inference that plants need more water when it is hot then when it is cool is that plants are like people. The excerpt says that plants are cooled by evaporating water. The excerpt also says that people sweat more in hot weather, so the reader can determine from this evidence that plants need more water when it is hot than when it is cool. The inference that is made is based on the explicit information in the excerpt. An inference is the best conclusion that you can make based on the information you have.

Determining the main idea of a passage

The main idea of a passage is what the passage is mostly about. It is the main point of the passage. Sometimes the main idea is stated in a passage by the use of a topic sentence either at the beginning of the passage or elsewhere. Sometimes the main idea may be found in the title of the passage. Oftentimes the main idea is not stated in the passage; the reader needs to determine it from the information or details in the passage. The main idea will become more and more obvious to a reader as detail after detail supports it. Some information in the passage may not be supporting, but most ideas and details will support the main idea. The main idea is filled out by the supporting details in a passage.

Decide what the main idea of the following excerpt is, "There are many processes in making coins."

> The United States Mint makes our money. The government chooses the designs. Artists make a clay model, and then they create a plaster model. A steel mold is made from this plaster model. A metal alloy is used for the coins. One machine punches out the coin and another imprints it with the design.

The information in the excerpt deals with the processes of making coins. It details what happens first, second, third, and so on when making a coin. The main idea is not stated in the excerpt, so the reader needs to put the details together to determine what it is. All of the details support the main idea being, "There are many process in making coins." All of the details describe these processes. The details about how coins are made are explicit: they are facts that can be checked. The central idea emerges from these facts and is shaped by the details that tell about the coin making processes. This is what supporting details do. They shape or tell more about the main idea so that the reader can tell what a passage is mostly about.

Objective summary

An objective summary of an informational text tells what the main idea of the text is and includes the important details. It tells what the text is mostly about and includes the most important supporting details. A summary should not include too much information; it is not a paraphrase of the information. It is important to select only the most important details to include. A summary should also be objective. This is achieved by focusing on the main idea rather than any opinions that might be in the text but that are not related to the main idea. It would also not include any personal opinions on the subject.

Read the summary and explain how to improve it.

> Edgar Degas was a great artist who broke with tradition and became an Impressionist. His paintings and sculptures are included in the collections of major museums everywhere. In his forties, his vision became poor and he worked more on sculptures because he could feel them. He died in 1917 at the age of 83. His father was a banker.

This summary is quite good. It has a main idea and includes some of the important details. The main idea is that Degas was a great artist. Supporting details include that his paintings and sculpture are included in collections of major museums as well as the fact that he had poor vision and turned to sculpting because he could feel the sculptures. While the information about his death is not perhaps the most important, it is of interest that he lived to the age of 83. The one glaring error with the summary is that it mentions the fact that his father was a banker. This does not directly relate to the main idea. It is not a supporting detail and is unimportant to the central thesis of the passage. It should be deleted.

Techniques used by authors

There are various techniques that authors use to make connections among and distinctions between individuals, ideas, or events. An author may choose to compare and contrast individuals, ideas, or events. This allows the reader to quickly see how something or someone is similar to or different from another thing or person. A second technique is through the use of analogies. An author may liken an idea, individual, or events by using analogies to show how they are similar and make her point clearer. An author might also put individuals, ideas, or events into categories to show how they are linked.

Read the excerpt and tell how the author makes connections between ideas.

> On the exterior it looked tidy and pleasant—a little log cabin with a fence around it. The lawn was cut close and the bushes were all tended to. No weeds in this yard. Inside was another story. The furniture was covered with dust. Huge spider webs dangled from the ceiling, and the floor was covered with dirt.

The author is comparing and contrasting the outside of a cabin with the inside. This is how the ideas are connected. Although the exterior looked tidy and pleasant, the interior was completely the opposite. It was dusty and dirty and had not been cleaned in a long time. Writers often link ideas. When a compare-and-contrast connection is made, the reader is quick to see the similarities and the differences between the two ideas or people being compared. Other ways to connect ideas is through categorizing. This technique is often used in scientific texts. Analogy is another way to connect ideas. This shows the relationship between two things or people so it is clearer to a reader.

Context clues

Context clues are an important resource when it comes to understanding the meaning of unknown words and phrases. Hints to the meaning of a word or phrase may be found in either the sentence in which the word or phrase is used or the sentences immediately before and after it. When determined the meaning of the word or phrase, substitute the synonym that you have for the unknown word or phrase. If it is still understandable, it is likely you have determining the meaning of the word. Figurative usage can also often be determined from the context of the text. Sometimes when reading technical text, it may be necessary to read more of the document to determine the meaning of a word.

Determine the meaning of "cordial" in the following excerpt.

> The salesperson smiled when the couple came into the store. She told them to take their time in choosing a ring. She chatted with them about their future plans. She was the most cordial salesperson they had ever met.

The excerpt states that the salesperson smiled. It says that she told them to take their time and that she chatted with them. Obviously the word "cordial" has a positive meaning based on these context clues. They seem to like the salesperson. She seems very pleasant. If you put the word "pleasant" in place of "cordial," the sentences make sense. Through this process it is possible to use context clues to help the reader understand the meaning of an unknown word. The same process can be used to decipher the meanings of unknown expressions or sayings.

Determine the meaning of "sense of foreboding."

> All day long Ron kept thinking about Sue. For some unknown reason he was worried about her. He had a strong sense of foreboding that something was about to go wrong in Sue's city. His fear was well-founded. Early the next morning, there was an earthquake. But fortunately, it was mild. Sue was shaken but unharmed.

The passage says that Ron kept thinking about Sue and that he was worried about her. Then it says that his fear was well-founded because there was an earthquake. From this the reader can determine what a "sense of foreboding" means. It means having a feeling that something bad will happen. If you substitute that phrase for "sense of foreboding," it makes sense. This process helps you understand what a word or phrase means. Always check for clues in the sentence and surrounding sentences to determine the meaning of unknown words or phrases.

Read the excerpt and determine the meaning of "contusion."

> Eli had fallen off the swing and his mother was very upset when she saw the swelling on his forehead. She rushed him to the emergency room. Dr. Vargas examined Eli and told his mother that it was just a contusion and nothing to worry about.

In this passage, the word "contusion" is a technical term. The reader can tell that it is a medical term because the doctor tells Eli's mother that is what he has. By reading through the passage, the reader will notice certain context clues that will help to determine the meaning of the word. Eli's mother saw a swelling on the child's head and took him to the emergency room. After the doctor examined the boy, she said the mother had nothing to worry about. The word "swelling" is key here. It suggests that "contusion" means a bump. If you replace "contusion" with "bump," the passage makes sense.

Figurative language

Figurative language is the use of ordinary words in a non-literal way or non-traditional manner. Figurative language is used by writers to expand their vision by creating images to make their writing more vivid and fresh. The literal meaning of a word or phrase is changed from its literal meaning to a figurative one. There are many different kinds of figurative language. A *simile* compares two things using the words "as" or "like." For example, "She was as clever as a fox." A *metaphor* compares two things without using the comparing words: "He was a fox when it came to getting out of a bad situation." *Personification* gives a thing or animal human traits. For example, "The fox cried out to him." When reading, look for non-traditional ways of using language that will contain hints to the meaning of the passage.

Which figurative language is used in the excerpt?

> We stood on the edge of the beach, a browned desert that offered no safe refuge, and watched the faltering ship struggling in the sea.

This is an example of a metaphor. The beach is likened to a browned desert that offered no safe refuge. They are compared without the use of the comparison words "as" or "like," so it is not a simile. The metaphor paints the beach in a negative way because it is compared to a desert with no safe refuge. The image adds vividness to the writing that would not exist if this image had not been added; it tells the reader what the author thinks of what is happening. It also suggests that something terrible is happening to the ship.

Denotative vs. connotative meaning of words

The *denotative meaning* of a word is the meaning that is found in a dictionary. It is the literal definition of a word. The connotative meaning is somewhat more subtle; it may also be listed in a dictionary, but after the literal meaning. The *connotative meaning* is what is suggested by or hinted at by a word, but not stated outright. The connotative meaning comes from the usage of the word. Its hidden meaning has come from personal experience. For instance, the words "lovely" and "exquisite" both mean "attractive," but "exquisite" suggests someone who is gorgeous or perfect-looking while "lovely" is less strong. When reading texts, you should always pay attention to words that have strong connotations because these words are a key to the author's opinion or point of view.

Read the following and explain the connotative meaning of the word "chef" and how it compares to "cook."
   I have always thought of myself as a chef, not a cook.

Both the words "chef" and "cook" can be defined as "someone who prepares food," but the word "chef" carries a higher status than "cook." It suggests someone who prepares food professionally rather than someone who merely prepares food as a necessity, such as for a family. The speaker obviously thinks highly of her cooking ability and prefers to think of herself as a professional. When you are reading, pay close attention to what a writer is suggesting through the choice of word. When you are writing, choose words carefully so that you don't depict something in a negative way by mistake. Utilize a dictionary and thesaurus to help you find the perfect word.

Analogy vs. allusion

An *analogy* is a relationship; it can be a relationship between two things, people, or even words. When reading a text, look for words that signify an analogy, such as "like" or "the same as." A writer might say that his situation is about the same as being stranded on a desert island. That becomes an image for what he feels. It helps make his frame of mind clearer. In the same way, an *allusion* will make a point clearer. Writers often allude to another circumstance or event to clarify their own experience. For instance, in the following sentence, the allusion to a fairy tale tells you what the writer is trying to say: "I'm working harder than Cinderella, but I don't see a prince in my future." The allusion to the famous fairy tale tells you that the speaker is not very happy.

Analyzing the structure of a paragraph

When reading a paragraph, a close study of the way in which is it structured is helpful. The reader should first look to see how the author begins the paragraph. Does she open the paragraph with a topic sentence or does she use some other technique, such as a humorous or dramatic statement, to begin the paragraph? If the second is true, does a topic sentence follow or do supporting details come next? If the topic sentence is at the start of the paragraph, supporting details would follow it. The last sentence is the conclusion. Some conclusions can be topic sentences, but that is not usual. The last sentence most often brings closure to the paragraph and signals the end. Paragraphs can also have an overall structure.

The structures of a paragraph include: a comparison and contrast structure, a cause and effect structure, a sequential structure, or a problem and solution structure. The structure of the paragraph depends a great deal on its main idea.

Determine the structure of this paragraph.

> The starfish hunts for clams in a strange way. When a starfish finds a clam, it wraps some of its arms around the clam. Then it pulls the clam open. After this, the starfish opens its mouth and pushes its stomach out of its mouth. The stomach goes into the clam shell and eats the clam and the starfish swallows its stomach again.

The paragraph opens with a topic sentence: "The starfish hunts for clams in a strange way." This sentence tells what the paragraph will be about. The other sentences are supporting details. They tell more about the main idea. The last sentence tells what happens at the end of the process of a starfish eating a clam. It provides closure. In determining the overall structure, the reader can use an elimination process. There is nothing to compare to the clam, so it is not a compare-and-contrast structure. There is no cause and effect structure indicated, nor is there a problem-and-resolution structure. The overall structure is sequential. The paragraph tells what happens in the order that it occurs.

Determining an author's point of view

The author's point of view is not always immediately clear. It could be stated clearly in many texts, but oftentimes the author does not want the reader to know exactly how he feels so a reader needs to discover it by the choice of words that an author uses, the information he includes, and any other relevant factors. It is important to read a text closely to determine what an author thinks about an event, person, topic or issue. Always check for any emotional statements that will give an idea of what the author is feeling. Look for any judgments an author may make about his topic, and piece together what you believe is the author's point of view.

How an author should acknowledge and respond to conflicting evidence or viewpoints

When discussing a controversial subject, an author has a duty to bring up both sides of an argument. The author may feel a certain way, but should still include opposing viewpoints in order to have a seemingly objective passage or essay. An author can, of course, refute the viewpoints but would need to use logical reasons why and cite any evidence that she wishes to include as testimony. In some cases, the author may not wish to side with either position, but merely to address the issues and give conflicting evidence so that the reader can form his own opinion about an issue.

Determine the author's point of view in the excerpt.

> Although flawed in some aspects, the play certainly kept the audience's attention, and there were cheers at the end. I look forward to Clemente's next play.

Based on what the author says in the excerpt, it would appear that he liked Clemente's play, even though he acknowledges some problems with it. He says as much by saying that, in spite of being "flawed" in some ways, the audience seemed to like the play because "there were cheers at the end." Then he goes on to say that he looks forward to Clemente's next play, which is the major suggestion that he, just like the audience, enjoyed the performance.

It is important to read a text closely to determine what the author's opinion is by what he says and suggests.

Determining the purpose of the text

While reading a text, you should always try to determine its purpose. To do so, ask yourself why the author wrote the text and what affect the writing has on you. Is the purpose to explain something or tell how to do something? Does the text try to persuade you of something? Perhaps the text is making an appeal to your emotions. The signs that a text is attempting to persuade you include an author offering an opinion and telling why she thinks that way. On the other hand, if a text is simply informative, it will have many facts that will give details about an event or person or a thing, but not try to persuade you of anything. Manuals that come with equipment are clearly not persuasive; they simply are instructive.

Describe the purpose of this excerpt.

> Bristlecone pines are remarkable. They are the longest-lived form of plant life in the world. These trees can live as long as 5,000 years. Some bristlecone pines standing today in the western United States were seedlings when the Egyptian pyramids were being built. They were mature trees by the year 1 AD.

The purpose of the excerpt is to inform. The way in which a reader can tell this is that the text has concrete facts and details about the bristlecone pines. It does not have any opinions, other than the obvious one, that "bristlecone pines are remarkable." The author of the excerpt is not trying to persuade the reader of anything other than that. And the details that she includes make the pines very remarkable. The formal language is to the point and the information is interesting. The writer wants people to learn about the bristlecone pines; she is not selling them nor is she asking people to protect them.

Advantages and disadvantages of using different media

There are advantages and disadvantages to using different media. Print and digital texts are portable so you can bring them with you wherever you go. That is a distinct advantage, but the disadvantages are many in comparison with video or multimedia. For instance, if you are interested in learning how to cook a certain dish, you can read a recipe, but seeing a video would be much more informative. If you are reading an autobiography of someone, then a multimedia presentation will allow you to hear recordings of a person or see an actor playing the person, and that may bring the book to life. This is the primary difference between print and performed versions.

How a movie version of Superman would be different from a comic book version

A movie version of Superman would be quite different from a comic book version because an actor would play the superhero and would speak as well as actually fly through the air. The comic book version would mean that the person would only be able to read the dialogue, not hear it. The pictures in the comic book would show what Superman is doing, but there would be no movement in the images as there would be in a movie. The movie could have special effects and special lighting to make the plot scarier or tenser, but such techniques are likely not as effective in a comic book version.

Importance of being a proficient reader of literary nonfiction texts by grade 8

It is of great importance that a student who reaches the end of grade 8 should be proficient in reading nonfiction texts because the texts that he will have to comprehend in the following years of school will be more difficult. These texts contain information on a variety of subjects that a student needs to master. Without being able to read well, a student may fall behind in his academic studies. Reading well is also the means of developing a good vocabulary. These skills will ultimately benefit the student not only in academic pursuits, but in all walks of life.

Writing

Producing clear and coherent writing

Every type of writing has its own characteristics, but to attain clear and coherent writing, it is necessary to plan what you will be writing about. You need to decide what your goal is; are you trying to write a narrative or are you writing to inform or persuade? After you have decided on your goal, you need to organize your material, especially in the case of nonfiction writing. You need to have a clear picture of your main ideas and supporting details. If you are planning to write a narrative, you need to pay attention to both developing your story in a clear and flowing manner and to creating believable characters through use of precise language including descriptions, dialogue and action. Another requirement is the establishment of a tone that is appropriate to the task, purpose, and audience. Finally, make sure your writing is grammatically correct and has no spelling errors.

Constructive criticism

You can work with your peers and adults to improve your writing. Have them read what you are writing and suggest ways to change it. An important part of the process is planning what you want to write. After you complete a first draft, you will need to revise your text. Editing the text comes next and you must develop a critical eye to make sure that the grammar and verb usage are correct and that you are using an active voice rather than a passive one. Sometimes you will find your writing fails to achieve its purpose. If that happens, you may have to start over and try something different. You may want to introduce a chart to make the material easier to understand, or change the ending to a story you are writing. Lastly, you need to learn how to assess if you have addressed your purpose and audience. Ask yourself whether the writing accomplishes what you want it to and if the language is suitable for the audience you want to reach.

Decide why the following passage needs revision and how to revise it

> Galileo was believing that the Earth moved around the Sun. They, the other teachers, did not believe that. He was sent to jail. Was being a brilliant mathematician. He was scorned by the other teachers at his university. They think him a foolish rebel. Now, we don't believe that he is considered a genius and a hero.

The writer of the passage has made a lot of grammatical mistakes. The style is not as formal as it should be and some sentences are almost incomprehensible. In the first sentence, an incorrect verb form is used. The second and fifth sentences seem to repeat the same information. The third sentence is not linked to the previous information. The fourth sentence does not have a subject. And the last sentence is a run-on. Here is one way to make those corrections:

Galileo believed that the Earth moved around the Sun. Because of this belief, he was sent to jail. Galileo was a brilliant mathematician. However, he was scorned by the other teachers at his university. In his own time, he was thought to be a foolish rebel. Now, he is considered a genius and a hero.

Now, the writing is much better organized and the mistakes are corrected.

Using the Internet

Online sources are invaluable tools. Writers can get works published at little or no cost as an e-book. There are other options available as well, such as editing and marketing services offered on many Internet sites. Some sites offer help with everything from style to grammar. Many sites can be used as credible research sources, where you find accurate and objective information for research projects and where you can compare information and ideas and how they may relate one to the other. Always cite all sources that you use from the Internet using the MLA (Modern Language Association) style as a guide. Additionally, the Internet has many sites where people can collaborate on projects. Chat rooms and topic websites are tools that allow an exchange of information as well as shared writing projects.

Conducting a short research project

When conducting a short research project to answer a question, draw up a list of keywords relating to the question. Use these words in a search engine to bring up websites that relate to the issue at hand. Use the most reliable websites for information to use in your research and be sure to keep track of the websites so that you can cite them in your text. While researching the subject, you will probably find related issues that would broaden the extent of your research project, so you may choose to come up with other keywords that would extend your research from its original scope. Make sure to draw from several sources when preparing your research paper. In that way, you can compare and contrast the information that is available.

When conducting research, your primary job is to list the kind of information you are looking for and then create a list of keywords to use for a search in multiple print and digital sources. Take extensive notes, noting the source that each bit of information comes from. Be sure to check on the reliability and credibility of each source. Journals, textbooks, magazines, and newspapers are all useful sources. Also, always verify how timely, accurate and credible your sources and information are. Dismiss any sources that seem questionable. When writing your report, you may paraphrase, but do not copy information down directly because that constitutes plagiarism. Use fresh language and attempt to rewrite the details and other information in your own language. Use the Modern Language Association (MLA) guidelines for all citations.

Analyze how the Bible is the basis of Andrew Lloyd Weber's musical Jesus Christ Superstar.

> Andrew Lloyd Weber's musical *Jesus Christ Superstar,* which dates from 1971, is loosely based on the last days of Christ's life from the Gospel and his relationship to Judas. However, many of the conversations and events included in the musical are not found in the Bible at all. *Jesus Christ Superstar* also makes use of songs and lyrics to bring the characters of Christ and Judas to life. It follows Christ's life from the time he and his disciples enter Jerusalem until the crucifixion, including Judas's betrayal of Christ. Judas is a very developed character in the musical and most of the action is the tension between Christ and him. Weber, like many other modern artists, makes use of the story from the bible, but uses it in a modern way so that it is appealing to modern audiences. Some of the music from the musical is still popular today.

Terri is researching a paper on hurricanes. Evaluate the following sources as to their reliability.

> http://www.nhc.noaa.gov/

http://en.wikipedia.org/wiki/

Tropical_cyclone

When doing research on the Internet, you need to be extremely careful that the website you are using to get facts and details about a subject is authorized and credible. The first source is a highly credible one. It is the National Weather Service National Hurricane Center. The information on this site would be totally credible because it is run by a component of the National Centers for Environmental Prediction (NCEP) at the Florida International University in Miami, Florida. All the information that you find there is accurate and credible because it is run by scientists in that field. The second source is not so credible. Wikipedia is not considered a credible source. It is not supervised in the way that a professional encyclopedia is. There are many mistakes that are made in their information. No academic group would accept it as a reliable source.

Making writing a habit

It is important that students become habitual writers. The more a student writes, the more he will improve his writing. Whatever the purpose for writing, students should be able to formulate their ideas into words. Some tasks will be shorter than others and require less work. A letter to a friend may not be a long undertaking, but a report will require more effort and time, including rewriting and editing as well as proofreading the finished paper. But whether the writing assignment is short or long, students need to find a way to become communicators with the written word. This means employing proper grammar and spelling as well as varied syntax to keep the reader interested.

Persuasive text

Introducing a claim

An excellent way to introduce a claim is to present evidence of its validity in a logical manner. The same can be true of distinguishing your claim from alternate or opposing claims. Logical evidence based on valid sources will give your claim strength. Central to organizing your reasons and evidence is doing excellent research and finding evidence that is based on facts and comes from experts in the field. Then the passage should be organized so that one idea flows from another and into the next. When writing, place your claim at the top and then list the reasons and evidence that support the statement. This will help you organize your passage logically.

When you present a claim, there should be supporting evidence that is reliable. Without credible evidence or sources, your argument will be weak. The evidence needs to be reliable and relevant and should cover every point that is made. It is vitally important that you do a great deal of research to develop your evidence. While researching, have a critical eye and anticipate what readers might say; this will help you to develop your claim thoroughly. It is not enough to research a claim on the Internet because many Internet sources are not reliable. When using the Internet, look for sites that are objective. Find experts that you can quote and use proven statistics. Make sure to present your information in a logical manner so that the reader can easily understand your argument.

Evaluating arguments and claims

When reading a persuasive essay, the reader will want to analyze and evaluate an argument and claims based on the validity of the evidence that is given. Claims are often made by authors, but it is important that these claims are backed with evidence. This evidence, however, must come from valid sources in order for it to be accepted. Sources include books that are written by experts on a subject, information from studies that are accredited, and Internet sources that are trustworthy. When analyzing a source, ask yourself if the source has any evidence of being an authority on the subject at hand.

Recognize irrelevant evidence

Claims are sometimes introduced but the evidence is not relevant to the subject of the text. It may be because the evidence does not come from a credible source, or because the evidence may have little to do with the claim. When evaluating evidence, ask yourself what relationship the evidence has to a claim. For instance, if a writer says that global warming is not occurring and then cites evidence from a study that is 25 years old, it is probably outdated and irrelevant to the claim. The reader should be aware of this possibility and disregard any irrelevant evidence. The reader should also be wary of any evidence that is not from a valid source.

Dealing with conflicting information

When confronted with information from two different texts that have conflicting information, the reader should decide whether the conflict is a matter of fact or interpretation. Often times, particularly in political texts, the same facts may be interpreted in different and conflicting ways. It is important for the reader to evaluate these facts and see if they are based on information that is credible. Then the reader must determine whether the various interpretations are supported by the facts. This is not always easy to do, but it is important for the reader to develop a critical eye for that very purpose.

Creating cohesion

The best way to create cohesion between claims, counterclaims and evidence is to organize your ideas and then write sentences explaining your reasons and evidence that follow your main ideas logically. Careful research will result in your argument being cohesive and easy to understand. Your claim and evidence must be clearly related to each other. Words that will indicate to the reader that the claim and evidence are related include "since," "because," "as a consequence" and "as a result." You can also utilize clauses to demonstrate a relationship between the reason and the effect. Consider the following sentence: "As a result of the following observations by scientist John Neal, more people have come to believe that a good night's sleep is necessary to being healthy." The sentence establishes causality between the reason and effect. When stating counterclaims, remember to use linking words such as "but" or "on the other hand" to indicate that an alternative claim will follow.

Maintaining a formal style

A formal style is used when writing essays, both persuasive and informative. This style helps the writer achieve objectivity and keep the language precise. Formal writing consists of complex words and sentences; sentence fragments should be avoided unless they are being used for a specific reason. The tone of the writing is serious. The third person is always used, not the first or second person. An active voice is preferred because it projects more energy than a passive voice. Contractions are not used in formal writing. Sentences should be grammatically correct, as should the spelling and punctuation. When writing, reread and edit your passage several times to improve it. Vary the kinds of sentences and make sure that your ideas follow a logical order as well.

Read the following passage and identify what style it is written in.

About two hundred years ago, world literature was growing rapidly. At that time, publishing books became profitable because people had more free time and turned to reading for entertainment. It was, however, quite a different reading compared to previous periods when books were created only for the few and not the everyman.

The excerpt is written in a formal style. The first thing to notice is that the third person is used for the viewpoint. The piece also has a serious tone and uses precise language. The sentences are complex and varied and no contractions are used. All of these details point to a formal style. If it were an informal style, the first or second person would be used, the tone would be more casual, and the language would be more generalized than is evident in this excerpt.

Importance of have a concluding statement

A concluding statement is important for a persuasive passage because it follows from and supports the argument that has been stated earlier in the passage. It should sum up the main points of the passage and give the reader a sense of completion and the passage a sense of closure. The purpose of the concluding sentence is to pull all aspects of the passage together and make sense of the ideas, evidence and details that have been included previously. The concluding statement should also be memorable because it will be last chance the writer has to convince the reader of his or her argument.

What kind of argument would the following sentence best conclude?

Physical activities help you become stronger, live longer, and make you happier.

The sentence would make a good concluding sentence for a passage about the reasons why one should adopt some form of physical activity. Arguments could include the benefits of different activities and why physical activity makes a person become stronger, live longer and be happier. The sentence was probably preceded with information on how to get started with a physical activity, such as being sure to check with a doctor before starting a new regimen, where a person can learn more about various forms of activities, and how to decide which activity is right for the reader. This sentence would provide closure for a passage of this type.

Informational or Explanatory Text

Introducing a topic

An informational or explanatory text should have an introduction to the topic that the text will feature. One way you can accomplish this is by using a topic sentence followed by details that support your thesis. Another tactic is to use a reference to a current event, even if your topic refers to something in history. Ideas should be organized in a logical manner, with supporting details coming after a main concept. Connections can be made between concepts by using connecting words such as "however," "since," and "as a result." Distinctions between ideas should also be made clear and can be signaled by words such as "but" or "on the other hand." Other organizational tips include choosing whether to include a specific relationship such as cause and effect, question and answer, or problem and solution.

Organizing ideas

There are many ways to present information so that it is easier to understand. One effective tool is headings. Each heading introduces a new concept or idea in a text and allows the reader to see, just by skimming, what the article is about and which points are being covered. Another useful tool is graphics. Graphics are extremely useful because they present a lot of detailed information in a visual form that is easy to understand. Instead of putting the information in a paragraph where it can be lost to the reader, it can be put into a graphic such as a chart or table that will make it much more approachable. Multimedia such as voice-over, videos or even movies are other excellent ways to present information; in this modern world, people respond very easily to this kind of presentation. Difficult material can be made much more enjoyable through the use of these tools.

Developing a topic

When developing a topic in an informational or explanatory text, it is vital that the text utilizes relevant facts that clearly support the main topic. After the introduction of the topic, claim or argument, concrete details and facts that are relevant should follow. The supporting details that are cited should be from reliable sources. At times, definitions of unfamiliar terms are appropriate. Quotations by experts in the field are also a good addition to a passage because they give credibility to the text and may make the subject more interesting to read about. The results of any research that might have been done would also be of interest. Examples or anecdotal incidents will also make a text more approachable.

Creating cohesion

The use of appropriate transition words helps to clarify the relationships between ideas and concepts and creates a more cohesive passage. A good writer knows that such words and phrases serve to indicate the relationship between ideas and concepts. Words or phrases that show causality between ideas include "as a result," "consequently" and "therefore." Words that show a compare-and-contrast relationship include "however," "on the other hand," "in contrast" and "but." When introducing examples of different concepts, words such as "namely," "for example" and "for instance" act as transition words. Transition words such as "foremost," "primarily," "secondly," "former" and "latter" can be used when showing the order of importance of ideas or concepts.

Decide how the following sentences could be written so that there is a better transition between the ideas.

It was time for the whales to breed. The whales were swimming south.

The author rewriting these two sentences should first understand their relationship to one another. There is a causality suggested here. The reason that the whales were swimming south is that it was time for them to breed. To combine the sentences, you need to use an appropriate transition word. In this case there are several options. The phrase "as a result" works well because it shows the causality between the two thoughts: "It was time for the whales to breed; as a result, the whales were swimming south." Other causality words such as "consequently" or "therefore" could also be used.

Importance of using precise language and domain-specific vocabulary

Writers of informational or explanatory texts need to use precise language and domain-specific vocabulary in order to express themselves clearly. General vocabulary words are not specific enough in many cases. A formal essay relies on the use of vocabulary that shows a mastery of a topic. Besides a main idea, details need to be included that are supplied by carefully chosen, precise and domain-specific language. Some of the terms will necessitate definitions, which can be included in the essay. While researching a subject, it is important to include technical vocabulary so that it can be used during the writing of the text.

Establish and maintain a formal style

Writers of informative or explanatory passages generally use a formal style because it has a greater sense of objectivity. The use of an informal style in informative or explanatory texts is not acceptable. A formal style always uses a third person. The formal style calls for complex and varied sentences. These will add a further tone of formality and depth to the subject. The use of a formal style shows the seriousness of a topic. Formal writing also includes clear and credible supporting details. Personal opinion rarely has a place in an informative or explanatory passage unless it can be justified in some way that is supported.

Rewrite the following so it is in a formal style.
> I've heard about volcanoes. I read that they are openings in the earth's surface. Lava, hot gases, and bits of rock come out of them. They are very forceful. I read that these volcanoes come from deep inside the earth.

Here is one way to re-write the passage:

Volcanoes are openings in the earth's surface from which lava, hot gases, and bits of rock erupt with great force. However, volcanoes begin deep within the earth.

Using the third person makes the passage more formal as well as more authoritative. Short and simple sentences are replaced with longer, more complex sentences, which make the passage more interesting to read. The vocabulary that is used is more sophisticated. Errors in grammar are also corrected. The final result is a text that is informed, precise and finely crafted.

Having a effective conclusion

Equally important to the beginning of an essay is an effective conclusion. A good concluding statement should review and sum up the information or explanation that precedes it in the text so that the reader can feel a sense of closure and completion. The conclusion should flow out of the information and bring the text to a logical end. Ideally the conclusion would review the most important points made in the presentation, the reasoning that is employed, and any supporting details that need to be remembered. A good conclusion should also allow the reader to reflect on what has been said, hopefully in a favorable light.

Narratives

Establishing a context

When writing a narrative, a context for the story has to be introduced; that context could consist of a description of a situation or a setting. A point of view also has to be established.

It could be introduced by a narrator and may or may not be the same as the author's. The points of view can be shown through dialogue or how the narrator reacts to or describes what characters do in the story. The characters will need to be drawn very clearly through their descriptions, what they do, and what they say. The author may hide his point of view in the characters' thoughts or actions. The narrator's point of view is usually more overtly seen in what is said in the narrative by the narrator.

Decide the character and point of view in the following passage.

> Alma Way stared straight ahead. Her long delicate face was pale. Her gloved hands, clutching the hymn book, trembled as she sang. The time for her solo was near. She felt panic rising within her but she took a deep breath. Then her voice rang out, clear as a bell. The congregation nodded admiringly.

The author has chosen to tell the narrative from the third-person omniscient viewpoint, which means the narrator is all-knowing. He introduces the character of Alma Way by describing her. He tells the reader a lot about her by describing how she is staring, that her face is pale and that her gloved hands clutched a hymn book. The narrator also tells us that she feels panic. The author has drawn a thorough picture of this woman for whom he seems to have some interest in. The reader would need to read on to learn more clues about what the narrator's and author's viewpoints are.

Sequence of events

The sequence of events in a narrative should follow naturally out of the action and the plot. Rather than being forced, the sequence should follow the natural flow of a dialogue or plot and enhance what happens in the story. The only time that sequence is not in the order that events happens is when an author decides to use the literary device called flashback. In this case the action does not flow in sequence but rather jumps back and forth in time. Events in a narrative are extremely important in helping the reader understand the intent or message of a narrative, which is why it is important to take note of the way in which the plot unfolds.

Techniques used by an author

Authors employ many techniques to make their narratives come alive and have meaning. Dialogue is an important one. It is often through the dialogue that a reader learns what is happening and what a character is like or is thinking. An analysis by the reader of the dialogue can yield important information about what is happening in the narrative. Equally important are the descriptions that an author uses to help the reader visualize a setting and what a character looks or acts like. Another important technique is pacing, which sets the stage for what is happening in a plot, whether the pace is slow and then quick. The pace is the rhythm of the story and can have a strong effect on creating tension in the story,

Transitions words

Transition words are important when writing a narrative so that the reader can follow the events in a seamless manner. They can also color the plot and the characters and show the relationships between experiences and events. Sequence words such as "first," "second," and "last" assist the reader in understanding the order in which events occur, which can be important to the flow of the plot. Words such as "then" or "next" also show the order in which events occur. "After a while" and "before this" are other sequence expressions. Transition words can indicate a change from one time frame or setting to another. "We were sitting on a rock near the lake when we heard a strange sound." At this point we decided to look to see where the noise was coming from by going further into the woods." In this excerpt the phrase "as this point" signals a shift in setting. It also shows the relationship between what was happening and what came next.

Using precise language

An author's precise language can help a reader gain insight into a story that an author has written. Precise language, including phrases and sensory language, helps the reader imagine a place, situation, or person in the way that the writer wishes. The details that an author uses to describe a setting or character will help bring a story to life and convey exactly what the author envisions. Details of what characters do, the setting, and the events in a narrative help create a lively and thought-provoking story. Sensory language helps convey the mood and feeling of the setting and characters and will bring insight into the theme of a narrative. When reading, take special care to understand the range of language that an author employs in order to better comprehend the meaning.

Read the excerpt and analyze its language.

> All through his boyhood, George Willard had been in the habit of walking on Trunion Pike. He had been there on winter nights when it was covered with snow and only the moon looked down at him; he had been there in the fall when bleak winds blew and on summer evenings when the air vibrated with the song of insects.

This excerpt is filled with precise and sensory language. The descriptions of walking on Turnion Pike "when it was covered with snow and only the moon looked down," of the "bleak winds" that blew and times that "the air vibrated with the song of insects" all contribute to bring the writing to life and allowing the reader to see what the author envisions in his mind by creating images through vivid and precise language. The description of the setting uses relevant details that help the reader understand something about George Willard. The language has the effects of drawing the reader into the story and revealing more about this character.

Role of a conclusion

The conclusion of a narrative is extremely important because it shapes the entire story and creates the theme that the author was attempting to convey. The conclusion of a narrative is the resolution of the problem that is faced by the characters. Some conclusions may be tragic, such as those in the many classic tragedies; other endings may be lighthearted, much in the style of classic comedies. Modern stories tend to have endings that are more complex than the clear-cut endings of classic literature. They often leave the reader without a clear sense of how a character fares at the end. Nonetheless, this element tells the reader that life is not always clear in its conclusions, which is a lesson that many writers strive to teach.

Betsy is writing a story about a girl who wants to be on the basketball team and works out every day to get in shape. She has written about the girl's feelings and the obstacles she has had to overcome. Now she wants to find a conclusion to the story. Describe what she should look for when trying to develop a good conclusion.

> Betsy should think about her character as though she were a real person because this seems to be a realistic story. She should think about what she wants to have as the story's theme. Does she want to show that hard work pays off? Or does she want to show that you cannot always get what you want even with hard work? In other words,

she has to decide whether the story will have a happy ending or not. Whatever kind of an ending she decides upon, the conclusion should bring the entire story to a fitting and appropriate end so that the reader has a sense of closure. It should follow the opening and the many events that happen so that there is a form to the story.

Speaking and Listening

Discussions

Group discussions

Group discussions are useful ways to brainstorm ideas and exchange information. They can lead to interactive learning and help students develop self-confidence when speaking. It is important to read the assigned text material carefully and study it until you have a thorough understanding of it and so that you will feel comfortable when discussing it. Think about what you want to stay about the issue and practice with a friend or family member. It is useful to talk in front of a mirror so that you become comfortable with discussion of the topic. Then you will be ready for the group discussion.

Preparing for a discussion

When studying material for a discussion, be sure to make notes about any information in the material that is evidence on the topic, text, issue or ideas under discussion so that you can use it as the discussion goes on. Prepare questions that you can ask which will promote discussion rather than a single-word answer. They contribute to a fruitful discussion. Use the evidence to draw the discussion into new areas that may produce a true exchange of ideas. During the discussion, try to avoid any conflict. If conflicts arise, the discussion is likely over. A group discussion should be an exchange of ideas, not a battle of egos.

Collegial discussions

Peers should decide on the rules of a collegial discussion before it begins, and all participants should observe those rules. A reference such as *Robert's Rules of Order* is a good resource to have on hand. The goals of the discussion and the time that will be spent on each topic should also be a consensus of the participants. Leaders of the discussion should be chosen, again by a consensus, and all participants would have to honor their lead. Discussion should not be open-ended, but rather reach the goal that has been identified within the deadline. Interruptions should not be tolerated. It is also essential that all students come to the discussion well prepared. If there is disagreement, the leader(s) should mediate until a consensus can be reached and facilitate the process until voting on any key issues can begin.

A large part of the success of collegial discussions is centered on the ability of participants to pose questions that connect to the ideas that are being presented. To do this, you will need to develop the ability to connect ideas and ask good questions that will illicit even greater discussion. This can be accomplished by being prepared for the material ahead of time and mastering the relevant evidence that is available. Another skill that can be developed is the ability to make observations from what is being said.

Acknowledging new information

The exciting part of a group discussion is that different people come to it with different information and evidence. It is the duty of each participant to listen politely to everyone's point of view and the evidence that they are presenting. When new evidence is cited by a participant that may go against the direction of the discussion, the first thing to do is to recognize it and privately evaluate the evidence. If the evidence seems reliable, it is important to acknowledge this fact so that the discussion can include the new points that are being made. Many participants become unnerved by information that they did not expect, but this is exactly the goal of a group discussion: to exchange ideas in a civilized manner.

Analyzing the purpose of information presented in diverse media and formats

When presented with information in diverse media and formats such as visual displays, oral presentations and others, it is important for the listener to analyze the purpose of the display or presentation as well as the reasons that it is being included. Some presenters may have hidden reasons for including the diverse media and formats. Oftentimes political presentations make use of diverse media and formats to try to sway the listener to vote for a particular person or issue. Sometimes they have a commercial purpose in that they want the listener to purchase something. Still others may have a social purpose; they may want the listener to give back to the community, for instance. The media and formats may be extremely appealing, so the listener would do well to see what evidence, if any, is being presented with the appeal.

Analyzing a speaker's argument

The ability to analyze a speaker's argument is an important skill both as a student and an adult. The first point to examine is the objectivity of the speech and whether there are hard facts supporting what the speaker says. Examine whether the use of evidence seems logical and credible. Make an attempt to judge the quality of the evidence and how clearly that evidence is presented. A good speaker uses rhetoric to persuade the audience. However, faulty reasoning arises from evidence that is irrelevant or not credible. Ask yourself if the speaker appears dogmatic or opinionated, or if he is clearly and demonstrably open-minded.

Presentations

Presenting claims with relevant evidence and valid reasoning

A good presentation of information should have a logical flow to it. It should address all of the important points that help focus the presentation and it should be organized in a coherent manner. The claims should be followed by relevant evidence and a display of valid reasoning. It is utterly important to choose details wisely so that the audience will have the most important details without having to wade through so much information that they become lost. The sources should be both cited and current. Important points most definitely can be repeated for effect. Using graphics at appropriate times can reinforce the argument(s) you are making. It is a good idea to practice making your presentation with friends or family and listen to their critiques.

Importance of using appropriate eye contact and body language

To become an effective speaker, certain skills should be mastered. Among these skills is learning to make and maintain eye contact with the audience or other participants when appropriate. Maintaining eye contact helps assure the audience that the presentation is believable and (hopefully) enjoyable. Eye contact makes the presentation personal, as though the speaker is speaking to someone directly. Smiling at times is also crucial to making a presentation successful, as is speaking in a clear voice that can be heard but is not unnecessarily loud. The speaker should use clear diction and pronunciation as well. These skills are the hallmark of an effective presentation.

Integrating multimedia and visual displays into presentations

The world is very sophisticated technically and when an audience comes to a presentation, it is a great advantage to have multimedia and visual displays that simplify difficult material and make the material more interesting. Something as simple as a chart may enhance the main claim that you are presenting to an audience. A PowerPoint presentation would probably be even more appealing to the audience and also has the added benefit of being able to objectify everything you say. Video and audio can also add strength to your claims and evidence by bringing information to life. While these are good extras, they do not make up for a faulty oral presentation, but they can enhance it greatly.

Adapting speech to a variety of contexts

Proper English can be very elegant when spoken correctly and it is extremely important for students to learn to speak with proper grammar. Of course, the kind of language you use in a speech will depend on your audience and what you hope to achieve. When you speak, make sure your verbs are used correctly and that you are aware of the use of active and passive sentences. Active and passive verbs can be used for good effect, depending on your need. When you speak, you need to learn to vary the form of sentences you use so that you include interrogative and imperative in addition to statements. Include verbs in the conditional and subjunctive mood in your speech. Practice your speech with a friend or family member so that you can be confident when you speak.

Decide why the word "waiting" is a gerund and not a participle in the following sentence.

Waiting for the test results was the hardest part for Vicki.

"Waiting" is a gerund in the sentence. It is the subject of the sentence. A *gerund* is a form of verb that ends in *–ing* and is used in the same way that a noun is. "Waiting for the test results" is a gerund phrase. A gerund phrase contains the gerund plus any complements and modifiers. In this case, "for the test results," is a prepositional phrase. The difference between a present participle and a gerund, both of which end in *–ing*, is that a present participle is used as an adjective and a gerund is used as a noun.

Language

Function of an infinitive verb form

An *infinitive* is a verb form that is usually preceded by the word "to" and can be used as a noun, an adjective, or an adverb. When "to" is used before a verb, it is not a preposition but part of the infinitive form of the verb. An example of an infinitive used as a noun is: "To exercise is important." In this example, "to exercise" is the subject of the sentence. An example of an infinitive used as an adjective is: "She had the wisdom to travel." The infinitive "to travel" modifies "wisdom." In the sentence, "We were happy to leave," the infinitive is an adverb that modifies the adjective "happy."

Moods of verbs

There are five moods that verbs can be formed in. The *indicative* is where a statement is made: "He leaves the house at 8 am." In the *interrogative*, a question is asked: "When does he leave the house?" The *imperative* is used for commands: "Leave the house at once!" In the *conditional*, a condition or wish is stated: "If he were smart, he would leave the house earlier." And in the *subjective*, a demand, recommendation, suggestion, or statement of necessity is made: "It is necessary that he be here on time." In the subjective and conditional forms, the verbs are distinctly different. For instance, in the example "If he were smart, he would leave the house earlier," the verb is a plural form rather than a singular form. In the sentence, "It is necessary that he be here on time" the correct verb form is "be" rather than "is."

Decide what error the following sentence has and how to correct it.

To patch an inner tube, it is necessary that the cyclist is prepared.

This sentence is incorrect grammatically because the verb form is not the right one. The sentence is a recommendation and therefore requires a subjective verb form. The verb forms "am, "is" and "are" are replaced in a subjective sentence with the verb form "be." The corrected sentence would read: "To patch an inner tube, it is necessary that the cyclist be prepared." The choice of an incorrect verb form is very common. Subjective verb forms are used in formal language but not as much in colloquial English. The subjective voice is used for a sentence that indirectly expresses a demand, recommendation, suggestion or statement of necessity.

Read the following sentence and correct it.

When the doctor turned on the instrument, a strange sound was heard.

This sentence is an example of an incorrect shift in the voice of the verb, something that is very common in colloquial English. The sentence starts out with an active verb, "turned on," and then shifts to a passive voice with "was heard." It can be corrected by rewording the second part of the sentence; the correct sentence reads: "When the doctor turned on the instrument, he heard a strange sound." Now both verb forms are in the active voice. The pronoun "he" agrees with its precedent "doctor." The active voice is preferred because it is stronger and more direct than the passive voice.

Read the following sentence and explain why and how it needs to be corrected.

Take a dose of medicine and then you should get some sleep.

This sentence shifts from an imperative verb mood to an indicative one. The verb moods in a sentence should match and these do not. There are two ways the sentence could be changed so the verb moods agree. Both verbs could be changed so they are in the imperative form. After doing this, the sentence would read: "Take a dose of medicine and get some sleep." You could also change both verbs to the indicative mood form: "You should take a dose of medicine and then you should get some sleep." Either sentence would be correct, although the second form is overly wordy. A shorter way of saying it would be: "You should take a dose of medicine and then get some sleep," where the second "you should" is understood.

Uses for the following punctuation marks: comma, ellipsis, and dash

Sometimes a comma, an ellipsis, and a dash are used to show that there should be a pause when text is read or spoken. A comma most often shows the need for a pause for before-and-after adverbs such as "therefore," "as a result," "however," "consequently" or before adverbs like "but," "while," and "so." A comma can be used after an introductory clause to show a pause as well. An ellipsis, or three small dots, can be used to show a pause in speaking when it is in the middle of a sentence that joins two ideas. A dash can also be used to show a pause when a parenthetical phrase is inserted into a sentence. However, the comma, ellipsis and dash are also used for other reasons, so do not assume that these are their only uses.

Correct the following sentence.

The news was however not as good as it might have been about the faltering ship.

There should be a comma before and after the word "however" to show that there is a pause. When reading a sentence like this, the voice naturally wants to pause around the word "however," which is the reason commas are placed around it. "However" is a conjunction and commas often set off conjunctions to allow for a pause. There are other reasons that commas are used as well. They are used to separate items on a list, for example. They are also used in the introduction and conclusion of a letter. The corrected sentence should read: "The news was, however, not as good as it might have been about the faltering ship."

Ellipsis

An ellipsis is used to show that a portion of a quote has been omitted. An ellipsis, which consists of three small dots, can come at the beginning, middle, or end of a quotation. The ellipsis should follow any existent punctuation in the quote. For example, the entire text of this quotation from John Donne is as follows: "No man is an island, entire of itself; every man is a piece of the continent, a part of the main." If you wished to omit a portion of the text, for instance the words "entire of itself," then you would punctuate it as, "No man is an island, ... every man is a piece of the continent, a part of the main." When omitting something that comes after a period, put the period first and then three dots.

Correct the spelling errors in the following sentence.

He put his foot on the accelerater and drove very quickely to the grandeose palace that the movie was using for it's setting.

The words that are misspelled are: "accelerater," which is spelled "accelerator"; "quickely," which is spelled "quickly"; "grandeose," which is spelled "grandiose"; and "it's," which should be "its." When writing, make sure to check in a dictionary to see how a word is spelled if you are unsure. Certain spelling rules will help, such as "I before E, except after C," (as in the word "receive") as well as "drop the final E" ("make" becomes "making,") and "double the last consonant" ("chop" becomes "chopping"). There are other skills that you can use to help you spell words correctly, such as sounding out words. By breaking longer words down into syllables, affixes and roots you may be able to determine the way a word is spelled. And in today's world, poor spellers are also assisted by software in word processing programs, such as spell check, which automatically lets you know if it suspects that a word is misspelled, although it is not 100 percent accurate.

Read the following sentence and change the verb to an active voice.
   The team was praised by the coach because of its record of wins.

To change the verb to an active voice the sentence should be rewritten as the following:

   The coach praised the team because of its record of wins.

The active voice is usually preferred because it is stronger. The passive voice can be used for effect, or might be used because no one knows who or what had caused an action. For instance, in the sentence, "The ball was broken," the reason the verb must be in the passive voice is that the reason the ball was broken is unknown. The passive voice is used when the writer does not want to emphasize the doer. It is frequently used in scientific texts.

Read the following sentence and analyze the verb.
   They spoke to her as if she were a child.

The verb form in the phrase "as if she were a child" is in the conditional form because it states a condition or a wish that is contrary to fact. Notice that this use of the conditional always requires the past tense. It also requires the plural form of the verb rather than the singular form. English speakers often make a mistake with the choice of verb. Although the conditional and subjunctive verb forms are not used a great deal in spoken English, they should be used when writing formal English.

Using context clues

Context clues are often found in the sentence that contains a new word or phrase as well as the sentences before and after it. A reader can often determine the meaning of an unknown word from these clues. For instance, a passage might say that the media have disseminated many foolish ideas about alligators. A reader might not be familiar with the word "disseminated," but then the passage goes on to say that some movies have implied that alligators spend their days waiting to attack an unsuspecting human being but, in fact, alligators usually feed on small animals like fish, snakes, and turtles, which live in or near the water and that it is very rare for an alligator to attack a human being. If you read this passage carefully, you can deduce that "disseminated" means "spread around." In this case, it means the spreading around of misinformation about alligators. Another helpful clue is that the word "disseminated" is in the position where a verb would go, so you would need another verb to take its place.

Use context clues to determine the meaning of "attribute" in the following excerpt.

> Some of the attributes of mammals are a backbone, warm blood, and the production of milk to nurse their young. In addition, almost all mammals bear living young. The platypus and the spiny anteater are exceptions. They lay eggs instead.

To determine the meaning of the word "attribute," the reader needs to analyze the rest of the sentence as well as the following sentences. It would appear that the excerpt is telling what mammals are like and what they have in common, with two exceptions. The excerpt says that mammals have a backbone, warm blood and that they produce milk to nurse their young. The word "attribute" as it is used is a noun, so you would look for another noun to replace it. If you substitute the words "trait" or "characteristic" for "attribute," the sentence seems to make sense. This is the way you can determine what a word or phrase means from the context clues that surround it.

Affixes and root words

A *root word* is a word before it is added onto. An *affix* is a prefix or suffix that is added onto a root word. Often, the affixes in the English language come from Latin or Greek origins. A *prefix* is added to the front of a root word and a *suffix* is added to the end of a root word. When you look at the meaning of a root word and the meaning of any affixes added to the root word, you can determine the approximate meaning of the word. For example, the root word "satisfied" means to be content with something. The prefix *dis-* means not. The reader can therefore determine that "dissatisfied" means to be not content with something.

Determine how the root and affixes of the word "precede" can help you determine its meaning.

You can determine the meaning of a word by studying its root and affixes. In the word "precede," the prefix *pre-* means "before." The root word "cede" comes from the Latin word "cedere," which means "to go." So the meaning of "precede" is fairly straightforward: it means "to go before." It is important for students to understand and study lists of prefixes and suffixes as well as root words and their meanings. This is a particularly good way to increase vocabulary and understand the origins of words. It is also useful when there is no context on which to determine the meaning of an unknown word.

Use general and specialized reference materials to find the pronunciation of a word

A print or digital dictionary can be used as a means to learn many things about a word. It will show the correct pronunciation of a word, tell its meaning, and its part of speech. The dictionary has a guide that shows how to sound out the words. It also lists all of the parts of speech that a word can be used as and the meanings it has in each form. In addition to the dictionary, the thesaurus is an extremely useful tool because it lists synonyms for all the various meanings a word can have, which helps you clarify the precise meaning as used in the context of the text you are reading. This means you can find other words to use in a report or text that mean the same as a word that may be used too often. Many books will have a glossary to help you with difficult or even technical words used in the text.

Anita was trying to verify the meaning of "brush" in the following sentence.

> She used her dictionary and found this.

brush (brŭsh) *n.* 1. A device with bristles. 2. A light touch in passing. 3. Contact with something dangerous. *v. tr.* 4. To clean with a broom. 5. To touch lightly in passing.

Choose the correct definition of "brush" from the following sentence.
   Peter brushed by me to get to the buffet.

The correct answer is meaning 5: "to touch lightly in passing." If you substitute that definition for the word, the sentence makes sense. Meanings 1, 2, and 3 are nouns and do not fit with the context of the sentence. Meanings 4 and 5 are verbs and "brush" is used here as a verb, so it would have to be one of these definitions. When considering which meaning is being used, always check for context clues in the sentence or in the sentences before or after the sentence in which the word is used. Dictionaries also tell you how to pronounce words and what part of speech they are.

Verbal irony and puns

Verbal irony is a figure of speech in which the intended meaning of a statement actually is different, and usually the opposite, of what is said. It is often sarcastic in nature, as in the retort of the mother whose child is playing with her food and says, "Do I have to eat this food?" The mother simply says, "No, of course you don't have to eat it. Just eat it tomorrow when you are really hungry." The mother does not mean what she says in reality, but she makes the point that the food will still be there for tomorrow. A *pun* is a play on words: "He said that he would like to axe me a question, but he didn't think it would be knife to butt in on me."

Relationships between words

The relationships between words can often enlighten a reader as to their meaning. For instance, you may come across the word "colossal" and not understand what it means, but then you are told that it means the opposite of "little," giving you a good clue to its meaning. The same is true of synonyms. If someone said a synonym for "minuscule" is "tiny," you would understand the meaning of the word at once. Analogies can also be useful for understanding the meaning of words. If you are told that "foot" is to "toe" as "paw" is to "pad," then you get an idea of what a pad is from the analogy.

Distinguishing between the connotations and denotations of words

The *denotation* of a word is the dictionary definition of the word. The *connotation* of a word is what the word suggests beyond its dictionary meaning. It is both the meaning that people associate with that word and a subjective interpretation of the meaning of the word. The denotation meaning is objective. For instance, the words "bullheaded" and "resolute" mean "firm" or "persistent." But "bullheaded" carries a negative connotation because it suggests someone who is very stubborn. "Resolute," on the other hand, has better connotations because there is no suggestion that the term means "unreasonable." When you read, you should pay attention to the language that a writer uses to describe something. Look for words that suggest something about a place or person that are not directly stated in the text.

Determine what the connotations are of the words "audacious" and "brash"
The connotations of "audacious" and "brash" are different. While they both technically mean "bold," the word "brash" has a more negative connotation because it suggests someone who

is hasty or even foolhardy. It could also suggest someone who is somewhat impolite. On the other hand, "audacious" has a slightly positive connotation because it means "daring" or "taking a chance" in a good way, possibly being brave. Writers often give their readers clues about characters, events, or places through the use of words that have strong connotations. It is important to study language used to describe things and people so such clues are not lost on the reader.

Improving comprehension

The acquisition of general academic and domain-specific words and phrases is especially important for success in academic endeavors. Without the ability to understand language at the high school level, a student will not be prepared for what he or she will encounter in the future, neither academically nor in life. Students must be familiar with domain-specific words and phrases if they hope to excel in a specific field. One excellent way to become proficient in language is to make lists of new words, use them in sentences, and learn to spell them. The glossary of a textbook is a good source for finding domain-specific words. Extended reading will allow the student to improve his or her vocabulary. Again, a good reader will try to understand the meaning of a word through context; should that fail, a student should find the precise meaning in a dictionary or glossary.

English Language Arts/Literacy Practice Test #1

Practice Questions

Read the following passage from Robert Frost's poem "The Road Not Taken" to answer questions 1-5.

Two roads diverged in a yellow wood,

And sorry I could not travel both

And be one traveler, long I stood

And looked down one as far as I could

5 *To where it bent in the undergrowth;*

Then took the other, as just as fair,

And having perhaps the better claim,

Because it was grassy and wanted wear;

Though as for that the passing there

10 *Had worn them really about the same,*

And both that morning equally lay

In leaves no step had trodden black.

Oh, I kept the first for another day!

Yet knowing how way leads on to way,

15 *I doubted if I should ever come back.*

I shall be telling this with a sigh

Somewhere ages and ages hence:

Two roads diverged in a wood, and I—

I took the one less travelled by,

20 *And that has made all the difference.*

1. What can be said about the author's tone in "The Road Not Taken"?
    a. He feels some remorse about his decision.
    b. He feels that he has accomplished something great.
    c. He feels that his path has been different.
    d. He feels that he should not have gone into the woods.

2. How does the point of view affect the tone of this poem?
   a. It creates a feeling of superiority in the reader.
   b. It causes the reader to feel slightly distanced from the scene.
   c. It makes the reader feel as if he/she is making the same decision.
   d. It causes the reader to feel as if he/she has no choice.

3. What is the main theme in this poem?
   a. Deciding which road to take while on a hike
   b. Making choices that may be different from others
   c. How to make the best of a decision in the past
   d. Wondering about the choices that others have made

4. What is the setting of this poem?
   a. The early morning, near some wood in the early or late spring
   b. The edges of a well-worn path near thick undergrowth
   c. Two paths that are near a more traveled one in the late morning
   d. The morning, in an autumnal forest with two walking paths

5. Which lines from this poem show a kind of irony?
   a. 16, 17, and 20
   b. 4, 5 and 6
   c. 6 and 8
   d. 18 and 19

Read the following passage from Heywood Broun's <u>The Fifty-First Dragon</u> to answer questions 6-10.

> OF all the pupils at the knight school Gawaine le Cœur-Hardy was among the least promising. He was tall and sturdy, but his instructors soon discovered that he lacked spirit. He would hide in the woods when the jousting class was called, although his companions and members of the faculty sought to appeal to his better nature by shouting to him to come out and break his neck like a man. Even when they told him that the lances were padded, the horses no more than ponies and the field unusually soft for late autumn, Gawaine refused to grow enthusiastic. The Headmaster and the Assistant Professor of Pleasaunce were discussing the case one spring afternoon and the Assistant Professor could see no remedy but expulsion.
>
> "No," said the Headmaster, as he looked out at the purple hills which ringed the school, "I think I'll train him to slay dragons."
>
> "He might be killed," objected the Assistant Professor.
>
> "So he might," replied the Headmaster brightly, but he added, more soberly, "we must consider the greater good. We are responsible for the formation of this lad's character."
>
> "Are the dragons particularly bad this year?" interrupted the Assistant Professor. This was characteristic. He always seemed restive when the head of the school began to talk ethics and the ideals of the institution.
>
> "I've never known them worse," replied the Headmaster. "Up in the hills to the south last week they killed a number of peasants, two cows and a prize pig. And if this dry spell holds there's no telling when they may start a forest fire simply by breathing around indiscriminately."

"Would any refund on the tuition fee be necessary in case of an accident to young Cœur-Hardy?"

"No," the principal answered, judicially, "that's all covered in the contract. But as a matter of fact he won't be killed. Before I send him up in the hills I'm going to give him a magic word."

"That's a good idea," said the Professor. "Sometimes they work wonders."

6. What is the best way to describe Gawaine's character?

    a. Fearless and excitable
    b. Careless and frigid
    c. Spiritual and careful
    d. Cowardly and apathetic

7. What is the meaning of "his better nature"?

    a. An increased sense of honesty
    b. A man's ignoble ideas
    c. A desire for propriety
    d. A man's nobler instincts

8. How does the Headmaster put the professor at ease about Gawaine?

    a. He tells him that Gawaine will only fight small dragons.
    b. He assures him that Gawaine's contract has not expired.
    c. He talks to him about the animals that have been killed by the dragons.
    d. He mentions that Gawaine will be given a magic word.

9. What would be a good question for the Headmaster to consider?

    a. Will Gawaine try hard to fight the dragons?
    b. Will Gawaine want to learn about fighting dragons?
    c. Will the professor let Gawaine learn about dragons?
    d. Will the professor teach Gawaine to fight the dragons?

10. Suppose that Gawaine's parents have him removed from the school. Would the Headmaster still want Gawaine to learn to fight dragons?

    a. No, he would be happy with the tuition payment.
    b. No, he would think that Gawaine would eventually return.
    c. Yes, because Gawaine is naturally very tall and strong.
    d. Yes, because Gawaine will get a special word for protection.

11. What might be one argument against the idea that "repetition is the mother of learning"? Write your answer below.
_____

12. If you needed to write an essay supporting the idea that "repetition is the mother of learning," what could one supporting detail be?
    a. Parents who repeat the same idea to their children hope that the children will eventually comprehend and understand it.
    b. Studies show that children who are exposed to different environments are able to adapt better to changes.
    c. Children who have heard the same topic presented in different ways show a better understanding of it.
    d. Scientists have claimed that repetition of a certain idea may have some bearing on the way children look at their worlds.

13. Which of the following statements should come after the topic sentence below?

"Video games are a part of every child's life, but scientists are now showing how damaging they may be."
    a. Some guys at a research place looked at why kids totally love games and they think that it has something to do with their thought patterns.
    b. Scientists got some kids to play games in a study and then told us all about it so they could show the importance of video games.
    c. Children and their parents always fight about games, and scientists know it—they just had to find a way to show it.
    d. In a recent study, scientists studied the brain scans of "gamers," or those who play video games regularly.

14. Write a thesis sentence for a paper titled "Safe *and* Fun: Extreme Sports"?
_____
_____
_____

15. Which of the following choices could best start an essay entitled "The Rise of the Robots: New Inventions for Everyday Life"?
    a. You may not take robots for granted right now, but if scientists have their way, you soon will. A whole host of new robotic helpers is on the way. Everything from washing your floors to helping grandma take a walk could be done by a new kind of robot.
    b. Robots are everywhere in science fiction, but are they soon to be an important part of life? Japanese engineers created the HRP-4C in 2009, a robot that can walk. The robot is designed to look like a young woman and can smile.
    c. Robots that look like people raise a lot of very important ethical questions—many that we don't even want to consider. Robots are really just machines, but the newer ones look so much like people that they may give you pause. Do robots have rights?
    d. Do you hate doing homework and taking tests? If scientists have anything to say about it, you may be able to get some help from a robot friend. The new robot tutors are designed to not only make schoolwork easier, but fun.

16. What quotation would most likely appear in a paragraph entitled "Hard Work Really *Does* Pay Off"?

    a. "And to get real work experience, you need a job, and most jobs will require you to have had either real work experience or a graduate degree. " (Donald Norman)
    b. "Don't go around saying the world owes you a living. The world owes you nothing. It was here first." (Mark Twain)
    c. "Men for the sake of getting a living forget to live." (Margaret Fuller)
    d. "O man you are busy working for the world, and the world is busy trying to turn you out." (Abu Bakr)

17. Read the sentence below. Which of the following choices should come next?

"Margie and George had known the water in the old fish tank was going to be too cold."

    a. Margie had known about the fish. They were all tropical fish that could swim very well and were quite beautiful.
    b. George, of course, had shown Margie the fish. They knew that the fish were different but didn't tell each other.
    c. The kinds of fish that go in cool water were not cheap. The kinds of fish that go in warm water were.
    d. In fact, it was so cold that it frequently cooled the house in the summer, and was certainly no place for tropical fish.

18. Which option best replaces the italicized words in the following sentence?

*"Angel **got into** her email account and read the homework message from her teacher."*

    a. went on
    b. signed up
    c. logged into
    d. got up

Read the following passage from Mark Twain's The Adventures of Tom Sawyer to answer questions 19-22.

[Tom Sawyer, a young boy who lives with his Aunt Polly, needs to whitewash the fence outside their house. Tom is not excited about spending the afternoon working hard.]

He got out his worldly wealth and examined it—bits of toys, marbles, and trash; enough to buy an exchange of WORK, maybe, but not half enough to buy so much as half an hour of pure freedom. So he returned his straitened means to his pocket, and gave up the idea of trying to buy the boys. At this dark and hopeless moment an inspiration burst upon him! Nothing less than a great, magnificent inspiration.

He took up his brush and went tranquilly to work. Ben Rogers hove in sight presently—the very boy, of all boys, whose ridicule he had been dreading. Ben's gait was the hop-skip-and-jump—proof enough that his heart was light and his anticipations high. He was eating an apple, and giving a long, melodious whoop, at intervals, followed by a deep-toned ding-dong-dong, ding-dong-dong, for he was personating a steamboat. As he drew near, he slackened speed, took the middle of the street, leaned far over to starboard and rounded to ponderously and with laborious pomp and circumstance—for he was personating the Big Missouri, and considered himself to be drawing nine feet of water. He was boat and captain and engine-bells combined, so he had to imagine himself standing on his own hurricane-deck giving the orders and executing them:

"Stop her, sir! Ting-a-ling-ling!" The headway ran almost out, and he drew up slowly toward the sidewalk.

"Ship up to back! Ting-a-ling-ling!" His arms straightened and stiffened down his sides.

"Set her back on the stabboard! Ting-a-ling-ling! Chow! ch-chow-wow! Chow!" His right hand, mean-time, describing stately circles—for it was representing a forty-foot wheel.

"Let her go back on the labboard! Ting-a-ling-ling! Chow-ch-chow-chow!" The left hand began to describe circles.

"Stop the stabboard! Ting-a-ling-ling! Stop the labboard! Come ahead on the stabboard! Stop her! Let your outside turn over slow! Ting-a-ling- ling! Chow-ow-ow! Get out that head-line! LIVELY now! Come—out with your spring-line—what're you about there! Take a turn round that stump with the bight of it! Stand by that stage, now—let her go! Done with the engines, sir! Ting-a-ling-ling!"

*Tom went on whitewashing—paid no attention to the steamboat. Ben stared a moment and then said: "Hi-YI! **<u>YOU'RE up a stump, ain't you!</u>**"*

No answer. Tom surveyed his last touch with the eye of an artist, then he gave his brush another gentle sweep and surveyed the result, as before. Ben ranged up alongside of him. Tom's mouth watered for the apple, but he stuck to his work. Ben said:

"Hello, old chap, you got to work, hey?"

Tom wheeled suddenly and said:

"Why, it's you, Ben! I warn't noticing."

"Say—I'm going in a-swimming, I am. Don't you wish you could? But of course you'd druther WORK—wouldn't you? Course you would!"

Tom contemplated the boy a bit, and said:

"What do you call work?"

"Why, ain't THAT work?"

Tom resumed his whitewashing, and answered carelessly:

"Well, maybe it is, and maybe it ain't. All I know, is, it suits Tom Sawyer."

"Oh come, now, you don't mean to let on that you LIKE it?"

The brush continued to move.

"Like it? Well, I don't see why I oughtn't to like it. Does a boy get a chance to whitewash a fence every day?"

That put the thing in a new light. Ben stopped nibbling his apple. Tom swept his brush daintily back and forth—stepped back to note the effect—added a touch here and there—criticized the effect again—Ben watching every move and getting more and more interested, more and more absorbed. Presently he said:

"Say, Tom, let ME whitewash a little."

Tom considered, was about to consent; but he altered his mind:

"No—no—I reckon it wouldn't hardly do, Ben. You see, Aunt Polly's awful particular about this fence—right here on the street, you know—but if it was the back fence I wouldn't mind and SHE wouldn't. Yes, she's awful particular about this fence; it's got to be done very careful; I reckon there ain't one boy in a thousand, maybe two thousand, that can do it the way it's got to be done."

"No—is that so? Oh come, now—lemme just try. Only just a little—I'd let YOU, if you was me, Tom."

"Ben, I'd like to, honest injun; but Aunt Polly—well, Jim wanted to do it, but she wouldn't let him; Sid wanted to do it, and she wouldn't let Sid. Now don't you see how I'm fixed? If you was to tackle this fence and anything was to happen to it—"

"Oh, shucks, I'll be just as careful. Now lemme try. Say—I'll give you the core of my apple."

"Well, here—No, Ben, now don't. I'm afeard—"

"I'll give you ALL of it!"

Tom gave up the brush with reluctance in his face, but alacrity in his heart. And while the late steamer Big Missouri worked and sweated in the sun, the retired artist sat on a barrel in the shade close by, dangled his legs, munched his apple, and planned the slaughter of more innocents. There was no lack of material; boys happened along every little while; they came to jeer, but remained to whitewash.

19. What is the main idea in the above selection?
    a. How Tom tricked others into doing his work.
    b. How Tom managed to get "wealthier" off his friends.
    c. How Tom finished the house painting in one afternoon.
    d. How Tom taught others about the value of work.

20. According to the passage, Ben says, "YOU'RE up a stump, ain't you!" Which of the following choices reflects a better way to express this sentence?
    a. "You're in a lot of trouble, are you?"
    b. "Your in trouble, aren't you?"
    c. "Your in a lot of trouble, ain't ya?"
    d. "You're in trouble, aren't you?"

21. Read the paragraph from the text and answer the question that follows.

> Tom swept his brush <u>daintily</u> back and forth—stepped back to note the effect—added a touch here and there—criticized the effect again—Ben watching every move and getting more and more interested, more and more absorbed.

Which word is a synonym for <u>daintily</u>?
- a. delicately
- b. furiously
- c. roughly
- d. vigorously

22. Read the excerpt from the text below and answer the question that follows.

> Tom surveyed his last touch with the eye of an artist, then he gave his brush another gentle sweep and surveyed the result, as before.

Select the answer that best defines the word "surveyed".
- a. rubbed on
- b. looked over
- c. redid
- d. complained about

Read the following passage from Douglas Fairbanks's <u>Live and Laugh</u> to answer questions 23-27.

> There is one thing in this good old world that is positively sure—happiness is for all who strive to be happy—and those who laugh are happy.
>
> Everybody is eligible—you—me—the other fellow.
>
> Happiness is fundamentally a state of mind—not a state of body.
>
> And mind controls.
>
> Indeed it is possible to stand with one foot on the inevitable "banana peel" of life with both eyes peering into the Great Beyond, and still be happy, comfortable, and serene—if we will even so much as smile.
>
> It's all a state of mind, I tell you—and I'm sure of what I say. That's why I have taken up my fountain pen. I want to talk to my friends—you hosts of people who have written to me for my recipe. In moving pictures all I can do is act my part and grin for you. What I say is a matter of your own inference, but with my pen I have a means of getting around the "silent drama" which prevents us from organizing a "close-up" with one another.
>
> In starting I'm going to ask you "foolish question number 1."—
>
> Do you ever laugh?
>
> I mean do you ever laugh right out—spontaneously—just as if the police weren't listening with drawn clubs and a finger on the button connecting with the "hurry-up" wagon? Well, if you don't, you should. Start off the morning with a laugh and you needn't worry about the rest of the day.

I like to laugh. It is a tonic. It braces me up—makes me feel fine!—and keeps me in prime mental condition. Laughter is a physiological necessity. The nerve system requires it. The deep, forceful chest movement in itself sets the blood to racing thereby livening up the circulation—which is good for us. Perhaps you hadn't thought of that? Perhaps you didn't realize that laughing automatically re-oxygenates the blood—your blood—and keeps it red? It does all of that, and besides, it relieves the tension from your brain.

Real laughter is spontaneous. Like water from the spring it bubbles forth a creation of mingled action and spontaneity—two magic potions in themselves—the very essence of laughter—the unrestrained emotion within us!

So, for me, it is to laugh! Why not stick along? The experiment won't hurt you. All we need is will power, and that is a personal matter for each individual to seek and acquire for himself. Many of us already possess it, but many of us do not.

*Take the average man on the street for example. Watch him go plodding along—no **spring**, no elasticity, no vim. He is in check-rein—how can he laugh when his **pep** is all gone and the sand in his craw isn't there any more? What he needs is spirit! Energy—the power to force himself into action! For him there is no hope unless he will take up physical training in some form that will put him in normal physical condition—after that everything simplifies itself. The brain responds to the new blood in circulation and thus the mental processes are ready to make a fight against the inertia of stagnation which has held them in bondage.*

23. What supports the author's premise that "happiness is... a state of mind"?
    a. Spontaneous laughter is useful.
    b. Those who try to be happy are happy.
    c. People should consider the "average man on the street."
    d. Physical exercise is needed for unenthusiastic people.

24. Which of the following is the best summary of the above selection?
    a. The mind is very important for determining happiness, and laughter is an important part of being happy.
    b. The mind controls the body, so if you can laugh about something every day, you will find that your blood circulation improves.
    c. The average person is interested in knowing how Douglas Fairbanks stays so positive, and he has written about how staying healthy is vital.
    d. Average people do not feel happy because they do not try to laugh or see things in a different way.

25. Read the paragraph below.
    I like to laugh. It is a tonic. It braces me up—makes me feel fine!—and keeps me in prime mental condition. Laughter is a physiological necessity. The nerve system requires it. The deep, forceful chest movement in itself sets the blood to racing thereby livening up the circulation—which is good for us. Perhaps you hadn't thought of that? Perhaps you didn't realize that laughing automatically re-oxygenates the blood—your blood—and keeps it red? It does all of that, and besides, it relieves the tension from your brain.

What does the author compare laughter to in the text?

___

26. Which of the following is closest in meaning to the word "pep"?
   a. Enterprise
   b. Apathy
   c. Liveliness
   d. Lethargy

27. Which of the following is closest in meaning to the word "spring," as used in the above selection?
   a. A season that follows the winter
   b. A sudden motion
   c. A violent change of mood
   d. A bounce

28. Which of the following introduces a claim that is not sufficiently supported by the evidence?
   a. That's why I have taken up my fountain pen.
   b. Take the average man on the street for example.
   c. Start off the morning with a laugh and you needn't worry about the rest of the day.
   d. Why not stick along? The experiment won't hurt you.

29. Which of the following would be the word that means "the study of the earth, its history, and its surface"?
   a. Geocaching
   b. Geography
   c. Geology
   d. Geometrics

30. According to the statement below, which of the following choices best matches the meaning of the underlined word?

   "The prince set two guards to cover the first watch, knowing that the enemy might come at any hour."
   a. A small device used to determine time
   b. To observe carefully
   c. A period of time for surveillance
   d. To wait on attentively

31. Which of the following dialogues best develop the action and characters in the story?
   a. Jane: "Ouch! I told you not to leave the cabinet door open! Now look what's happened—again! My other knee is cut now."

   Peter: "It's your own fault. If you were paying attention, it wouldn't happen. Besides, who told you to go in there? Nosey, are we?"
   b. Jane: "Ouch! That really hurt! I can't believe that it happened again. It's like the same things over and over again."
   Peter: "Well, it's really your own fault. I don't see how it has to do with someone else. You really need to be more careful."
   c. Jane: "Ouch! Why is that cabinet door open again! I thought I closed it yesterday. As a matter of fact, I am sure that I closed it yesterday."
   Peter: "You probably just forgot to do it. After all, you are pretty absent-minded."
   d. Jane: "Ouch! Did you leave that cabinet door open? I just hit my knee on it and now I have a big cut there. It really hurts!"

Peter: "Is your knee hurt? Why aren't you more careful? Now both of your knees are cut."

32. Which of the following sentences probably comes next?

"First, Janice rolled up her sleeves and glanced at the clock."
    a. She counted backwards two hours establishing the starting point for her story.
    b. Finally, she counted backwards two hours to establish the starting point for her story.
    c. Second, she was counting backwards for two hours to establish the starting point in her story.
    d. Then, she counted backwards two hours to establish the starting point for her story.

33. Which of the following endings could be a satisfactory conclusion to the story?

> *Bob and Peter went skateboarding in the park on Saturday, even though it was supposed to rain. The boys had been skating for a few hours when the rumble of thunder sounded and raindrops began to fall. The boys gathered up their boards and were running towards the park exit when they heard a cry. "Help! My brother has fallen in the water and I can't reach him! Help! He can't swim!" Bob pulled Peter's sleeve and pointed towards the pond. A frightened girl ran back and forth by the edge of the water.*

    a. Bob and Peter take their skateboards home and call the police to see if they can help the boy in the park.
    b. Bob and Peter go skateboarding around the pond to see if the boy is really in trouble before heading home.
    c. Bob goes home while Peter goes to the pond to see if the girl needs some help. He tries to rescue the boy from the pond.
    d. Bob and Peter go to the pond to help the boy. They use their skateboards to help pull the boy from the water.

34. Which of the following sentences is written correctly?
    a. Peter and Jaime slowly opened the door peered into the shadows and then ran across the room.
    b. Peter and Jaime slowly opened the door, peered into the shadows, and then ran across the room.
    c. Peter and Jaime slowly opened the door, peered into the shadows, and then ran across the room
    d. Peter and Jaime, slowly opened the door, peered into the shadows, and then ran across the room.

35. Come up with a word that would fit in the blank.

"Of all the puppies in the kennel, James chose the chubbiest one. He didn't even look at the dogs who were _____ and underfed. He had no interest in a sickly animal."

_____

36. Pretend you read an article in a science journal that showed organic food is healthier than non-organic food. One of your classmates, Charlie, then said organic food is not healthier for you. Which of the following statements could you make in a group discussion on this topic?

    a. "Although Charlie disagrees, I believe organic food is healthier for you than non-organic food because of a research article I read in a science journal."
    b. "I believe that organic food is healthier for you than non-organic food is, but Charlie says otherwise."
    c. "Even though Charlie says that organic food is not healthier for you than other foods, I think that his conclusion is based on his own opinion."
    d. "Charlie mentioned that he does not believe that organic food is healthier for you than other kinds of food, but it's quite obvious that he is guilty of an *ad hominem* attack."

37. Which part of the sentence is the infinitive?

"To persevere in the face of hardship shows great character."

    a. face of hardship
    b. in the face of
    c. To persevere
    d. shows great character

38. Which of the following sentences contains an error in grammar usage or punctuation?

    a. My best friend, Xavier, went fishing on Saturday and hiking with his family on Sunday.
    b. Angelina and Ruby, were excited about there new clothes; they decided to wear them.
    c. Mr. Johnson saw the reaction in the test tube; he added more sodium to see what would happen next.
    d. Sabina, frightened out of her wits, picked up the phone and dialed 9-1-1.

39. Susan is revising a research paper that she wrote for English class. She decided that the underlined words below are too informal.

We should all remember the sacrifices that have been made to ensure our freedoms, and we should take full advantage of those freedoms. If we don't, those who died to ensure that all Americans have the right to life, liberty, and the pursuit of happiness will have died in vain. I hope that my <u>age group</u> will be the first of many to make voting one of our most important and treasured rights once again.

Rewrite the third sentence, replacing the underlined words with a more formal term.

_____
_____
_____

40. The following sentence contains an error.

If people do not stand up and choose their own leaders, someone else will do it for them: and who knows what those leaders will stand for?

Rewrite the sentence below, correcting the error.

_____
_____
_____

Answers and Explanations

1. A: Line 16 reveals that the author will be talking about this moment later with a sigh. There is nothing in the poem to indicate that the author has done something great or that he should have not gone into the woods. While he does seem to say that his path has been different than others, that does not describe the tone of the poem.

2. C: The first person point of view makes the reader feel as if he/she is involved in making the same decision. The other choices involve other points of view: an omniscient reader would feel superior or even a little distanced from the scene. The reader also has a clear choice, so letter D would not be a good selection.

3. B: This is because the writer mentions there are two paths, and one seemed more worn than the other, showing it was more often used by travelers. The other choices involve reading too much into the poem.

4. D: The setting is laid out in lines 1 and 11.

5. A: Frost uses a type of irony called "verbal irony" here, and shows us his feelings by using expressions that go against what the literal words say.

6. D: Gawaine is said to be tall and sturdy, but would run away and hide at the smallest sign of trouble.

7. D: "His better nature" is a common way of talking about a person's deeper character.

8. D: Letter A is not mentioned in the text, and the other choices do not directly answer the question.

9. B: Considering Gawaine's character, this is the only choice that makes sense because it is well known that Gawaine is cowardly and the professor doesn't seem to know much about dragons.

10. A: This can be inferred from the text:

"Would any refund on the tuition fee be necessary in case of an accident to young Cœur-Hardy?"

"No," the principal answered, judicially, "that's all covered in the contract."

11. "Just saying something over and over again doesn't mean that a student really understands it." This statement is one possible example, as it supports a counter-argument in a clear manner.

12. C: While the other choices may be supporting details, this is the best choice because it is most closely related to the main topic.

13. D: This choice makes the most sense because the topic sentence involves how scientists are showing that video games are bad for children.

14. "Extreme sports like snowboarding, skateboarding, and mountain climbing can all be done in a safe and exciting manner." This would be one example of a good thesis statement for a paragraph about "Safe *and* Fun: Extreme Sports".

15. A: This is the only choice that directly reflects all aspects of the essay's title.

16. B: The other choices may mention work, but they do not support the idea that hard work is good and profitable.

17. D: This is the only choice that correctly uses a transition and addresses every part of the first sentence and provides new information for creating a story.

18. C: This bit of computer jargon refers to someone signing into or gaining access to their email account or profile page on the Internet.

19. A: This is one of Twain's most oft-repeated passages, and while the other choices are true, they are not giving a good summary of the paragraphs.

20. D: This sentence shows how the quote should be written. The other selections all involve grammar errors.

21. A: Tom was painting daintily or delicately. These words are synonyms and both describe him painting in an easy, gentle pattern.

22. B: In this sentence, Tom was looking over his work with the eye of an artist.

23. B: This is the only statement that directly gives support to the idea that "mind over matter" is a part of the will. The other choices are points from the paragraph used to illustrate other ideas.

24. A: While all of the choices have some truth to them, this is the only one that gives a complete summary of the selection.

25. He compares it to a tonic. This is directly stated in the text: "I like to laugh. It is a tonic. It braces me up…"

26. C: "Liveliness" is another word for pep. Enterprise refers to an endeavor, apathy is indifference, and lethargy is sluggishness.

27. D: While the other choices may have something to do with the word "spring," they do not give the correct definition for the word as it is used in the selection.

28. C: The other choices either do not make a specific claim, or make a claim that the author tries to support. There is no support to show that the reader won't have to worry about the rest of the day.

29. C: "Geo" is the Greek prefix for "Earth" and "-logy" is a suffix meaning "the study or discourse."

30. C: The other choices are other meanings for the word "watch," but option C is the only choice that makes sense in the context of the sentence.

31. A: This choice provides the best character and story development.

32. D: The other choices do not use the transition words correctly nor follow the pattern set in the first sentence.

33. D: Based on the boys' behavior in the story, this is the only choice that makes sense. Bob and Peter are not afraid to take risks (they go to the park despite warnings of rain) and they stop to listen to the cries for help.

34. B: This shows the clearest expression of the main idea and is grammatically correct.

35. A good word to go in the blank would be "skinny", or any synonym of skinny.

36. A: This choice acknowledges your classmate's ideas while explaining and supporting your own claims in a polite fashion.

37. C: This is the infinitive, which is simply the basic form of a verb.

38. B: This sentence is incorrect because it has the wrong word for "their" (there). It also has a misplaced comma (after "Ruby").

39. A more precise word for "age group" would be "generation".

40. C: This sentence has two independent clauses that include "and" as the coordinating conjunction. Adding a comma between "them" and "and" is the most appropriate change to make the meaning of the sentence clear. A semicolon or a colon would not be correct here, and would cause the reader to be confused. The corrected sentence would read:

If people do not stand up and choose their own leaders, someone else will do it for them, and who knows what those leaders will stand for?

English Language Arts/Literacy Practice Test #2

Practice Questions

1. Which of the following is similar to the claim made by Albert Einstein that "Sometimes one pays most for the things one gets for nothing"?
    a. "The best things in life are free."
    b. "Easy come, easy go."
    c. "There's no such thing as a free lunch."
    d. "A stitch in time saves nine."

2. Which of the following best provides detailed support for the claim that "seatbelts save lives"?
    a. A government website containing driving accident information
    b. A blog developed by one of the largest car companies in the world
    c. An encyclopedia entry on the seatbelt and its development
    d. An instant message sent out by a famous race car driver

3. Which of the following choices best completes the sentence below?

It is better to see the doctor for routine, yearly check-ups instead of waiting until you are experiencing a big health problem _____.

    a. After which the doctor may be able to provide a referral to a specialist.
    b. Because the doctor can usually spot problems before they get too big to handle.
    c. Since a routine visit is more likely to happen at least once a year.
    d. So the best thing to do is to contact your doctor when you need help.

4. Which of the following would best support the argument that people cause global climate change?
    a. The average global temperature has increased 1.5 degrees Fahrenheit since 1880.
    b. Common greenhouse gases include carbon dioxide and water vapor.
    c. Most of the greenhouse gases today come from burning things like coal and other fossil fuels for energy.
    d. The average person breathes out about 1.0 kg of carbon dioxide every day, while the average cow produces about 80 kg of methane.

5. Write a good concluding sentence for a paragraph entitled "The Best Books You've Never Read"?

_____

_____

6. Which of the following choices would be the best beginning for an essay on "Scientists Debate: Global Climate Change"?

    a. The Earth is heating up. The polar ice caps are melting and whole species are going extinct while governments and scientists argue over rules and regulations.
    b. The argument seems to be about whether climate change is really happening and if so, who causes it. Some scientists argue that people are causing the change.
    c. If the Earth heats up, what will our new world look like? Scientists who have dedicated their lives to understanding climate change have projected a series of scenarios that could happen.
    d. While few people can understand all of the issues related to climate change, one thing is sure: scientists do not agree. There seem to be several different views on how to look at climate change data.

7. Fill in the blank with the correct transitional phrase in the following passage?

However, not all scientists agree that people are causing climate change. _____, the famous "Hockey Stick" graph, which showed a huge spike in the global temperature, is being debated.

_____

8. Which of the following words best replaces the underlined term?

Newer "green" products are available, such as recycled boxes, non-toxic baby toys, and cloth grocery bags.

    a. plant-based
    b. garden-like
    c. environmentally-friendly
    d. climate-altered

9. Which sentence best completes the following paragraph?

There are many issues our school faces. First, there is a problem with litter. Students do not seem concerned about the garbage and paper they leave on the floors and desks. Second, there are issues with the class schedules. Students have to run from one end of the campus to the other in just a few minutes. Finally, the library does not have enough money to buy books. All of the money for the library had to be used to fix the water damage from the storm.

    a. The worst of these three problems is the issue with litter, since class schedules and library problems are not as serious.
    b. These three problems are the most serious issues that need to be addressed because they affect the daily operation of the school.
    c. The day-to-day operations of our school will be affected if we do not address one of these problems.
    d. Litter, class schedules, and library problems all contribute to the problems our school is facing, and they are quite serious.

Read the following selection from H. G. Well's book, The Time Machine, to answer questions 10-13.

[The Time Traveller is talking to his friends. He has just explained that while three dimensions— length, breadth, and thickness— are typically accepted, a "fourth dimension" should also be considered.]

*'Well, I do not mind telling you I have been at work upon this geometry of Four Dimensions for some time. **Some of my results are curious.** For instance, here is a portrait of a man at eight years old, another at fifteen, another at seventeen, another at twenty-three, and so on. All these are evidently sections, as it were, Three-Dimensional representations of his Four-Dimensioned being, which is a fixed and unalterable thing.*

'Scientific people,' proceeded the Time Traveller, after the pause required for the proper assimilation of this, 'know very well that Time is only a kind of Space. Here is a popular scientific diagram, a weather record. This line I trace with my finger shows the movement of the barometer. Yesterday it was so high, yesterday night it fell, then this morning it rose again, and so gently upward to here. Surely the mercury did not trace this line in any of the dimensions of Space generally recognized? But certainly it traced such a line, and that line, therefore, we must conclude was along the Time-Dimension.'

'But,' said the Medical Man, staring hard at a coal in the fire, 'if Time is really only a fourth dimension of Space, why is it, and why has it always been, regarded as something different? And why cannot we move in Time as we move about in the other dimensions of Space?'

The Time Traveller smiled. 'Are you sure we can move freely in Space? Right and left we can go, backward and forward freely enough, and men always have done so. I admit we move freely in two dimensions. But how about up and down? Gravitation limits us there.'

*'Not exactly,' said the Medical Man. **'There are balloons.'***

'But before the balloons, save for spasmodic jumping and the inequalities of the surface, man had no freedom of vertical movement.'

'Still they could move a little up and down,' said the Medical Man.

'Easier, far easier down than up.'

'And you cannot move at all in Time, you cannot get away from the present moment.'

'My dear sir, that is just where you are wrong. That is just where the whole world has gone wrong..."

10. Which of the following best summarizes the above selection?
    a. It is a conversation involving the age of men and space.
    b. It is a conversation about the nature of time and space.
    c. It is a dialogue from two friends about their medical ideas.
    d. It is a dialogue from two colleagues about time and distance.

11. As referred to in paragraph 6 above, what is a synonym for the word "spasmodic"?
_____

12. In this question, you will need to compare the paragraph that appears in question 10 (about school issues) to the selection from <u>The Time Machine</u> above. How do the structures of the texts contribute to their functions? Choose the best answer.

    a. <u>The Time Machine</u> text uses dialogue to pull the reader along to a conclusion, while the straight-forward listing of issues in question 10 keeps the reader's focus by being short and to the point.
    b. <u>The Time Machine</u> text uses an explanation of gravity to interest the reader, while the straight-forward listing of issues in question 10 keeps the reader's focus by explaining some solutions.
    c. <u>The Time Machine</u> text is short and comes to the point, while the listing of issues in question 10 allows for the reader to think more deeply about the ideas.
    d. <u>The Time Machine</u> text uses complex arguments to make a simple point, while the straight-forward listing of issues in question 10 does not allow for the development of arguments.

13. What effect does the point-of-view in this story have on its development?
    a. It makes the reader feel intelligent.
    b. It creates confusion.
    c. It builds suspense.
    d. It develops a feeling of contentment.

Read the passage below from <u>How it Works</u> by Archibald Williams to answer questions 14-17.

> *The most familiar form of electricity is that known as magnetism. When a bar of steel or iron is magnetized, it is supposed that the molecules in it turn and arrange themselves with all their north-seeking poles towards the one end of the bar, and their south-seeking poles towards the other. If the bar is balanced freely on a pivot, it comes to rest pointing north and south; for, the earth being a huge magnet, its north pole attracts all the north-seeking poles of the molecules, and its south poles the south-seeking poles. (The north-seeking pole of a magnet is marked N., though it is in reality the south pole; for unlike poles are mutually attractive, and like poles repellent.)*
>
> *There are two forms of magnet—permanent and temporary. If steel is magnetized, it remains so; but soft iron loses practically all its magnetism as soon as the cause of magnetization is withdrawn. This is what we should expect; for steel is more closely **compacted** than iron, and the molecules therefore would be able to turn about more easily. It is fortunate for us that this is so, since on the rapid magnetization and demagnetization of soft iron depends the action of many of our _____ mechanisms.*

14. Which of the following words best completes the blank?
    a. molecular
    b. north-seeking
    c. pole-like
    d. electrical

15. Which of the following is closest in meaning to the word "compacted" in the above selection?
    a. Pledge
    b. Efficient
    c. Compress
    d. Dense

16. What might be the best way to help students understand the concept of magnetism?
    a. Have them read the encyclopedia entry on temporary magnets and permanent magnets and then ask students to write an essay on the topic.
    b. Ask students a series of discussion questions related to electricity and then ask them how they would explain it to others.
    c. Show them a short movie that demonstrates the movement of the molecules in a piece of magnetized metal and then have students participate in group discussions.
    d. Allow students to examine a graphic illustrating the electro-magnetic spectrum and draw conclusions about magnetism based on the graphic representation.

17. Which of the following sentences best develops the idea of how magnetism can be tested?
    a. If steel is magnetized, it remains so; but soft iron loses practically all its magnetism as soon as the cause of magnetization is withdrawn.
    b. The most familiar form of electricity is that known as magnetism.
    c. When a bar of steel or iron is magnetized, it is supposed that the molecules in it turn and arrange themselves with all their north-seeking poles towards the one end of the bar, and their south-seeking poles towards the other.
    d. If the bar is balanced freely on a pivot, it comes to rest pointing north and south; for, the earth being a huge magnet, its north pole attracts all the north-seeking poles of the molecules, and its south poles the south-seeking poles.

Read the following statements to answer questions 18 and 19.

Lisa Grant: "Schools should make students wear uniforms. Everyone would look the same. Students would be able to respect each other based on their ideas and character because they would no longer be judged by their appearance."

Joe Smith: "Students should not have to wear uniforms. Clothing is an important part of self-expression. Taking away that method of expression is suppressing that student's rights."

18. What idea do both of the students seem to agree upon?
_____
_____
_____

19. Which of the following statements could NOT provide support for BOTH arguments?
    a. A number of local school districts have recently implemented dress codes.
    b. School administrators have been in talks with parents over the issue of uniforms.
    c. Students have reported that school uniforms are costly and typically ill-fitting.
    d. Several groups of students have been organized to discuss uniform dress codes.

Read the following selection from <u>Ten American Girls From History</u> by Kate Dickinson Sweetser to answer questions 20-23.

[Clara has begun her work of ministering to soldiers on the front lines of the civil war. Her tireless efforts and care have taken her to some of the most horrific battles of the war]

> *Clara Barton!—Only the men who lay wounded or dying on the battle-field knew the thrill and the comfort that the name carried. Again and again her life was in danger— once at Antietam, when stooping to give a drink of water to an injured boy, a bullet whizzed between them. It ended the life of **the poor lad**, but only tore a hole in Clara Barton's sleeve. And so, again and again, it seemed as if a special Providence protected*

her from death or injury. At Fredericksburg, when the dead, starving and wounded lay frozen on the ground, and there was no effective organization for proper relief, with swift, silent efficiency Clara Barton moved among them, having the snow cleared away and under the banks finding famished, frozen figures which were once men. She rushed to have an old chimney torn down and built fire-blocks, over which she soon had kettles full of coffee and gruel steaming.

As she was bending over a wounded rebel, he whispered to her: "Lady, you have been kind to me ... every street of the city is covered by our cannon. When your entire army has reached the other side of the Rappahannock, they will find Fredericksburg only a slaughter-pen. Not a regiment will escape. Do not go over, for you will go to certain death."

She thanked him for the kindly warning and later told of the call that came to her to go across the river, and what happened. She says:

"At ten o'clock of the battle day when the rebel fire was hottest, the shells rolling down every street, and the bridge under the heavy cannonade, a courier dashed over, and, rushing up the steps of the house where I was, placed in my hand a crumpled, bloody piece of paper, a request from the lion-hearted old surgeon on the opposite shore, establishing his hospitals in the very jaws of death:

"'Come to me,' he wrote. 'Your place is here.'

"The faces of the rough men working at my side, which eight weeks before had flushed with indignation at the thought of being controlled by a woman, grew ashy white as they guessed the nature of the summons, ... and they begged me to send them, but save myself. *I could only allow them to go with me if they chose, and in twenty minutes we were rocking across the swaying bridge, the water hissing with shot on either side.*

"Over into that city of death, its roofs riddled by shell, its every church a crowded hospital, every street a battle-line, every hill a rampart, every rock a fortress, and every stone wall a blazing line of forts.

"Oh, what a day's work was that! How those long lines of blue, rank on rank, charged over the open acres, up to the very mouths of those blazing guns, and how like grain before the sickle they fell and melted away.

"An officer stepped to my side to assist me over the débris at the end of the bridge. While our hands were raised in the act of stepping down, a piece of an exploding shell hissed through between us, just below our arms, carrying away a portion of both the skirts of his coat and my dress, rolling along the ground a few rods from us like a harmless pebble in the water. The next instant a solid shot thundered over our heads, a noble steed bounded in the air and with his gallant rider rolled in the dirt not thirty feet in the rear. Leaving the kind-hearted officer, I passed on alone to the hospital. In less than a half-hour he was brought to me—dead."

She was passing along a street in the heart of the city when she had to step aside to let a regiment of infantry march by. At that moment General Patrick saw her, and, thinking she was a frightened resident of the city who had been left behind in the general exodus, leaned from his saddle and said, reassuringly:

"You are alone and in great danger, madam. Do you want protection?"

With a rare smile, Miss Barton said, as she looked at the ranks of soldiers, "Thank you, but I think I am the best-protected woman in the United States."

20. What can be inferred from the fact that the men's faces turned "white" in the underlined sentence?
    a. The men were afraid that Clara would be seriously hurt or killed by going to help.
    b. The men had not wanted Clara to tend to them or order them around when she first arrived.
    c. The men were terrified of the coming war and wanted Clara to escape with them.
    d. The men did not want to be moved to the hospital on the other side of the bridge.

21. Which of the following might be a good title for the above selection?
    a. Clara Barton: "The Angel of the Battlefields"
    b. "The Angel of the Civil War"
    c. Civil War Nurses and the Work of Clara Barton
    d. "When the Fighting Was Over: Clara Barton, Civil War Hero"

22. Why does the author mention the instances when Clara's life had been in danger on the battlefield?
    a. To show that Clara was an unwilling participant in the initial war effort.
    b. To help the reader picture how Clara seemed to not really be a part of the battle.
    c. To compare how many battles she lived through with how many armed men had not.
    d. To illustrate how battles were turned through the care she provided.

23. Which of the following best explains why the author referred to one of the soldiers as "the poor lad"?
    a. She wanted to show that the man had little or no material belongings.
    b. She wanted to build sympathy for the young man who died.
    c. She wanted to show that the soldier had only been a young boy, not a man.
    d. She wanted to create an image in the mind of the reader about the soldier.

24. Which of the following choices is closest in meaning to the sentence below?

[Mercutio, Romeo's friend, utters this line shortly after receiving a fatal wound in this selection from William Shakespeare's Romeo and Juliet.]

"Ask for me tomorrow and you shall find me a grave man."

Act III, scene i: lines 97 – 98
    a. If you question about me tomorrow, you can see that I am not being silly.
    b. Please ask about my tomb tomorrow when you visit.
    c. I am very serious about this issue, so please come and see me tomorrow.
    d. I will not survive this incident and will be dead by tomorrow.

25. The following definition is from the dictionary. According to this definition, what part of speech goes with the part of the definition "one chosen or set apart"?
    [From Chambers's Twentieth Century Dictionary (part 2 of 4: E-M), by Various]

Elect, e-lekt', v.t. to choose out: to select for any office or purpose: to select by vote.—adj. chosen: taken by preference from among others: chosen for an office but not yet in it (almost always after the noun, as 'consul elect').—n. one chosen or set apart.—n. **Elec'tion**, the act of electing or choosing: the public choice of a person for office, usually by the votes of a constituent body: freewill: (theol.) the exercise of God's sovereign will in the predetermination of certain persons to salvation: (B.) those who are elected

---

26. Which of the following choices would be the best way to start a paragraph about a teenager in a futuristic society?

    a. M'ze looked at all of the robots in the street. Each one looked exactly the same as the other. M'ze sighed and pressed a button nearby. The Servicebots began to disappear as he rose higher into the sky.

    b. M'ze gazed out moodily over the rows of mechanical Servicebots. He pressed the button on his jet pack and rose above the mob to join the flock of workers already in the skies above. "It's time to go to work," he sighed, his mind turning to his mother's tiny hospital cubicle.

    c. M'ze blew his hair out of his eyes again and let his gaze fall on the rows and rows of robots before him. "Servicebots. 'Servicebots to serve you!'" he sneered at the soundless, sightless mass. He pressed a button on his jet pack.

    d. M'ze thought about the robots. The Servicebots were lined up in front of him like an army. "If only my mom could see me now. She would be really disappointed." M'ze pressed a button nearby. If you saw him, you would have thought of a thin, blue bird with sad eyes.

27. Mary Shelley's <u>Frankenstein</u> begins with a story about a young man on a journey and his subsequent meeting with Dr. Frankenstein. The same kind of technique is also used in Emily Bronte's <u>Wuthering Heights</u>. What kind of narrative technique does this represent?

    a. Narrative hook
    b. Deus ex machina
    c. Cut-up technique
    d. Frame narrative

28. Which of the following choices best fill the empty blanks in the sentences below?

_____, Darwin did not have access to all the startling facts we do today. _____, he didn't know about DNA, which was discovered in 1953. Secondly, he did not have access to the large number of well-researched materials modern science offers."

    a. "Chiefly" and "As a result"
    b. "Although not likely" and "In the first place"
    c. "Although this may be true" and "Serendipitously"
    d. "In consideration of this" and "Firstly"

Read the following passage from Charles Dickens's <u>David Copperfield</u> to answer questions 29 and 30.

I was born at Blunderstone, in Suffolk, or 'there by', as they say in Scotland. I was a posthumous child. My father's eyes had closed upon the light of this world six months, when mine opened on it. There is something strange to me, even now, in the reflection that he never saw me; and something stranger yet in the shadowy remembrance that I have of my first childish associations with his white grave-stone in the churchyard, and of the indefinable compassion I used to feel for it lying out alone there in the dark night, when our little parlour was warm and bright with fire and candle, and the doors of our house were—almost cruelly, it seemed to me sometimes—bolted and locked against it.

29. How does the author convey sadness?

    a. Through the discussion of his birth in Scotland half a year after his father had passed away.
    b. Through his description of his memories about his father's grave stone and its location.
    c. Through his reflection in the mirror and his memories about his first explorations into the darkness.
    d. Through his recollection that he had been born six months after his father died, and that his father had never seen his own son.

30. Which of the following could serve as a concluding sentence in the above paragraph?

    a. I rarely thought of my father after I visited his grave, since his absence in my life had little to do with my future.
    b. The grave stone was set in such a very lonesome place, and I couldn't bear the thought of going to visit it.
    c. It was true, I missed my poor father dearly, even though I never really laid eyes on him, nor him me.
    d. My father's own thoughts must have dwelt on similar issues, even though I was but a child and he was but a specter.

31. Read the citation below. Which part of it is incorrect?

Schwartz. Michael J. What's New Is Old. New York: Classic Books, 2012.

32. In the book Roll of Thunder, Hear My Cry, the theme of independence and self-respect is one part of the story. It can be seen in the way Cassie's family interacts with others. Which of the following classic stories also has a similar theme?

    a. A Separate Peace by John Knowles
    b. My Antonia by Willa Cather
    c. The Fall of the House of Usher by Edgar Allen Poe
    d. Wuthering Heights by Emily Bronte

33. Which of the words in the sentence below is the past participle?

"Logan had already forgiven Marianne for telling his secret, and so when he was presented with a chance to treat her in kind, he simply did what he did best—he kept his mouth shut."

    a. telling
    b. forgiven
    c. and
    d. treat

34. Which of the following choices is an example of the passive voice?

    a. My friends told me about the new rules.
    b. The computers at school are much faster than the ones at the library.
    c. Her cell phone has been stolen.
    d. His hat is on the chair.

35. Which of the following sentences is written correctly?
    a. Maya, my pet bird, can say "hello" in three languages.
    b. Jason, Peter Alice and Soojin all wanted to visit the new museum.
    c. Don't forget to bring your violin—music book—and music stand to the lessons.
    d. If you bring all of the supplies for the project I will provide the workspace.

36. What word goes in the blank?

Hours of research and preparation went into the initial _____ of the computer data, and even then, the scientists called for others to investigate their claims independently.
    a. anaylsis
    b. anaylses
    c. analysis
    d. anlysis

37. What is the speaker emphasizing in this quote?
    [from JFK's Inaugural Speech: 1961]

    "And so, my fellow Americans, ask not what your country can do for you; ask what you can do for your country.

    "My fellow citizens of the world, ask not what America will do for you, but what together we can do for the freedom of man."

    a. He's focusing on the fellowship of his countrymen.
    b. He's focusing on the freedoms of man.
    c. He's emphasizing the ability of the nation.
    d. He's emphasizing the actions of the listeners.

38. Which of the following best completes the sentence?

The dark cavern was gently illuminated by the glow from the golden cage. The heroes ventured closer to the odd light from the ancient artifact. Wen gripped his twin swords tightly as Druj raised his battle axe. The willowy sorceress, still deeply enveloped in her cloak, allowed her _____ hands to extend out from it.
    a. pale
    b. pasty
    c. cadaverous
    d. anemic

39. What might be the purpose of the following selection?

[Martin Luther King, 1963: I Have a Dream.]
    Let us not wallow in the valley of despair, I say to you today, my friends.

And so even though we face the difficulties of today and tomorrow, I still have a dream. It is a dream deeply rooted in the American dream.

I have a dream that one day this nation will rise up and live out the true meaning of its creed: "We hold these truths to be self-evident, that all men are created equal."

I have a dream that one day on the red hills of Georgia, the sons of former slaves and the sons of former slave owners will be able to sit down together at the table of brotherhood.

I have a dream that one day even the state of Mississippi, a state sweltering with the heat of injustice, sweltering with the heat of oppression, will be transformed into an oasis of freedom and justice.

I have a dream that my four little children will one day live in a nation where they will not be judged by the color of their skin but by the content of their character.

I have a dream today!

    a. Instructive: To create a more positive feeling about the future of the constitution
    b. Social: To make the audience think about their own dreams and desires
    c. Commercial: To illustrate how unfair the system in Mississippi and Georgia is
    d. Political: To show how things appear to be now and what he hopes will happen

40. Which of the following sentences is correct?

    a. The telescope accomplished amazing feats of enlargement, from showing the pock-marked face of the moon to the many moons of Saturn.
    b. The children all said that they had the best times of their life when they all lived together in the little two-bedroom bungalow.
    c. The study found that children frequently chose to use the entire bag of marshmallows for their hot cocoa.
    d. The astronomers found that the planets were following regular patterns and the philosophers argue about the nature of those paths.

Answers and Explanations

1. C: This is the only answer that addresses the idea in the quote. The idea that nothing is really ever free is part of the idea Einstein was trying to communicate.

2. A: The government website would publish the most recent data on seatbelt information, like how many people wore seatbelts in the accident and how many survived. Choices B and C are more likely to be opinion-based. Choice C is tempting, but it would not give someone the most up-to-date information.

3. B: This is the best choice because it provides more information about why it is important to see the doctor for regular checkups.

4. C: This choice shows how greenhouse gases are released from burning coal and other fuels, which people need for power. The first, second, and third choices are facts, but don't show a relationship to the main idea.

5. A good concluding sentence might read: In conclusion, the best thing you can do for yourself is to skip the bestsellers and get your hands on some classics. This tells you how to go about finding the books in the paragraph.

6. D: This is the best choice because it takes a look at the idea that scientists are not in complete agreement about climate change. Choice A takes only one position, option B is more of a detail that may go in the essay, and choice C is about a different topic.

7. "For example" would be the best transition, because the sentences clearly show that an example of something is coming next.

8. C: "Green" products refer to those items that are safer for the environment and people than other conventional items.

9. B: This is the best choice because it mentions the main idea (issues the school faces) and provides an adequate summary of the topic.

10. B: The two men are talking about four possible dimensions and their ability to move through them.

11. The definition of spasmodic is occurring or done in brief, irregular bursts. Some good choices for synonyms would be "occasional" or "intermittent".

12. A: It is the only answer that correctly describes the two passages. Option B incorrectly identifies an explanation of gravity as the key point of interest in the passage from <u>The Time Machine</u>, option C incorrectly describes <u>The Time Machine</u> as being like the speech and vice versa, and option D incorrectly describes the concept of time travel as simple and the presentation of simple issues as inarguable.

13. C: It builds suspense because the Time Traveller already knows about the outcome of his experiments with time travel, and he is only leading his audience along by explaining the thought process behind it.

14. D: Electrical is the correct answer because the entire selection is about electricity and magnetism. Nothing in the article mentions molecular tools (A); and the other two answers, which come from the text, would not make sense in this context.

15. C: "Compress" is the word closest in meaning to the underlined word, "compact." While a compact can be a pledge or refer to something that is neat, efficient, or dense, these meanings cannot be derived from the context.

16. C: This would be the best way to help students see how the molecules move in metal. Then, a discussion afterwards would help to clarify any issues raised about the movie. The first choice only relies on text to explain this difficult concept, which may not be enough for most learners. Only asking discussion questions about magnetism would probably not help students if they did not already have a good idea of how magnetism worked, and seeing a representation of the electro-magnetic spectrum would not be able to explain how magnetism operates.

17. D: This is the best choice because it provides a simple description of how someone can see magnetism in his or her daily life.

18. Both of the speakers are arguing over the respect due to an individual, but they are going about it in different ways.

19. C: This detail would only really support the argument against wearing school uniforms, while the other three choices could all appear as details in support of either side of the argument.

20. A: The text indicates that the "rebel fire was hottest, the shells rolling down every street, and the bridge under the heavy cannonade" and "a courier… placed in my hand a crumpled, bloody piece of paper, a request from the lion-hearted old surgeon on the opposite shore, establishing his hospitals in the very jaws of death." Both of these indicate that the soldiers knew that the situation was dangerous, no place for an unarmed lady.

21. A: The text mentions Clara being helpful during several battles. While she may have helped throughout the Civil War, it is not the topic here. Choice C focuses more on other nurses in the war, and Choice D doesn't make sense because Clara was on the battlefield when the fighting was taking place.

22. C: The author mentions that men had been shot while Clara lived, demonstrating an interesting dichotomy of her life: the unarmed nurse who was protected on the battlefield, while the armed men did not seem to be.

23. B: While the other choices may have some truth to them, there is no evidence in the text that the soldier had little money (A). Options C and D give only partial answers.

24. D: Shakespeare uses a pun, or a play on words, to add character to the scene.

25. It is a noun. This is stated explicitly in the definition as "n" for noun.

26. B: This choice is the best because it establishes a consistent point of view, a tone, a period of time, and engages the reader with two questions: why M'ze hates work and why his mother is in the hospital.

27. D: A frame narrative uses a main story to tell either one or more stories inside of it. Frankenstein is a multiple frame story: the young man tells of Dr. Frankenstein, who in turn also tells the Monster's tale.

28. B: This is the only choice that makes sense. The sentences indicate that there may have been something that Darwin understood, a negative appears in the sentence (…Darwin did not have access…). The second sentence is obviously following a counting pattern (Secondly).

29. B: This answer comes directly from the text and the narrator's elaborate description of his father's grave and its location. Options A and D describe things that the passage does not describe as vividly, while option C makes reference to a mirror reflection that is not mentioned in the passage at all.

30. A: This is the only choice that mentions how the author feels about his father and follows the sadness and longing in the narrative. Choices A and B do not adequately show how the author feels towards his father and choice D refers to the supernatural, which is not mentioned here.

31. According to MLA format there should be a comma in between the last name and first, not a period. It should read: *Schwartz, Michael J. What's New Is Old. New York: Classic Books, 2012.*

32. B: My Antonia by Willa Cather is a classic tale about a woman's life in Nebraska with a strong theme of personal independence and self-respect.

33. B: The past participle usually goes along with "have" or "had."

34. C: The other choices all use the active voice. For sentences involving the passive voice, the subject of the sentence gets the action from the verb.

35. A: The other sentences either incorrectly use the comma (if at all) or the dash.

36. C: "Analysis" is the correct spelling of the word.

37. D: The emphasis on the actions of the listeners can be seen in the words "ask," "you," and "do."

38. A: While all of the words are similar in meaning, the passage refers to the people as "heroes" and the sorceress as "willowy," so the connotation of the word should be positive.

39. D: This is taken from Martin Luther King Jr.'s "I Have a Dream" speech in 1963. In it, King discussed important issues of race and equality while expressing his hope for the future.

40. C: This choice shows the appropriate mood and tense. The other examples show mixed constructions (A) and errors in the construction (B) or verb tense (D).

How to Overcome Test Anxiety

Just the thought of taking a test is enough to make most people a little nervous. A test is an important event that can have a long-term impact on your future, so it's important to take it seriously and it's natural to feel anxious about performing well. But just because anxiety is normal, that doesn't mean that it's helpful in test taking, or that you should simply accept it as part of your life. Anxiety can have a variety of effects. These effects can be mild, like making you feel slightly nervous, or severe, like blocking your ability to focus or remember even a simple detail.

If you experience test anxiety—whether severe or mild—it's important to know how to beat it. To discover this, first you need to understand what causes test anxiety.

Causes of Test Anxiety

While we often think of anxiety as an uncontrollable emotional state, it can actually be caused by simple, practical things. One of the most common causes of test anxiety is that a person does not feel adequately prepared for their test. This feeling can be the result of many different issues such as poor study habits or lack of organization, but the most common culprit is time management. Starting to study too late, failing to organize your study time to cover all of the material, or being distracted while you study will mean that you're not well prepared for the test. This may lead to cramming the night before, which will cause you to be physically and mentally exhausted for the test. Poor time management also contributes to feelings of stress, fear, and hopelessness as you realize you are not well prepared but don't know what to do about it.

Other times, test anxiety is not related to your preparation for the test but comes from unresolved fear. This may be a past failure on a test, or poor performance on tests in general. It may come from comparing yourself to others who seem to be performing better or from the stress of living up to expectations. Anxiety may be driven by fears of the future—how failure on this test would affect your educational and career goals. These fears are often completely irrational, but they can still negatively impact your test performance.

> **Review Video:** <u>3 Reasons You Have Test Anxiety</u>
> Visit mometrix.com/academy and enter code: 428468

Elements of Test Anxiety

As mentioned earlier, test anxiety is considered to be an emotional state, but it has physical and mental components as well. Sometimes you may not even realize that you are suffering from test anxiety until you notice the physical symptoms. These can include trembling hands, rapid heartbeat, sweating, nausea, and tense muscles. Extreme anxiety may lead to fainting or vomiting. Obviously, any of these symptoms can have a negative impact on testing. It is important to recognize them as soon as they begin to occur so that you can address the problem before it damages your performance.

> **Review Video:** 3 Ways to Tell You Have Test Anxiety
> Visit mometrix.com/academy and enter code: 927847

The mental components of test anxiety include trouble focusing and inability to remember learned information. During a test, your mind is on high alert, which can help you recall information and stay focused for an extended period of time. However, anxiety interferes with your mind's natural processes, causing you to blank out, even on the questions you know well. The strain of testing during anxiety makes it difficult to stay focused, especially on a test that may take several hours. Extreme anxiety can take a huge mental toll, making it difficult not only to recall test information but even to understand the test questions or pull your thoughts together.

> **Review Video:** How Test Anxiety Affects Memory
> Visit mometrix.com/academy and enter code: 609003

Effects of Test Anxiety

Test anxiety is like a disease—if left untreated, it will get progressively worse. Anxiety leads to poor performance, and this reinforces the feelings of fear and failure, which in turn lead to poor performances on subsequent tests. It can grow from a mild nervousness to a crippling condition. If allowed to progress, test anxiety can have a big impact on your schooling, and consequently on your future.

Test anxiety can spread to other parts of your life. Anxiety on tests can become anxiety in any stressful situation, and blanking on a test can turn into panicking in a job situation. But fortunately, you don't have to let anxiety rule your testing and determine your grades. There are a number of relatively simple steps you can take to move past anxiety and function normally on a test and in the rest of life.

> **Review Video:** How Test Anxiety Impacts Your Grades
> Visit mometrix.com/academy and enter code: 939819

Physical Steps for Beating Test Anxiety

While test anxiety is a serious problem, the good news is that it can be overcome. It doesn't have to control your ability to think and remember information. While it may take time, you can begin taking steps today to beat anxiety.

Just as your first hint that you may be struggling with anxiety comes from the physical symptoms, the first step to treating it is also physical. Rest is crucial for having a clear, strong mind. If you are tired, it is much easier to give in to anxiety. But if you establish good sleep habits, your body and mind will be ready to perform optimally, without the strain of exhaustion. Additionally, sleeping well helps you to retain information better, so you're more likely to recall the answers when you see the test questions.

Getting good sleep means more than going to bed on time. It's important to allow your brain time to relax. Take study breaks from time to time so it doesn't get overworked, and don't study right before bed. Take time to rest your mind before trying to rest your body, or you may find it difficult to fall asleep.

> **Review Video:** The Importance of Sleep for Your Brain
> Visit mometrix.com/academy and enter code: 319338

Along with sleep, other aspects of physical health are important in preparing for a test. Good nutrition is vital for good brain function. Sugary foods and drinks may give a burst of energy but this burst is followed by a crash, both physically and emotionally. Instead, fuel your body with protein and vitamin-rich foods.

Also, drink plenty of water. Dehydration can lead to headaches and exhaustion, especially if your brain is already under stress from the rigors of the test. Particularly if your test is a long one, drink water during the breaks. And if possible, take an energy-boosting snack to eat between sections.

> **Review Video:** How Diet Can Affect your Mood
> Visit mometrix.com/academy and enter code: 624317

Along with sleep and diet, a third important part of physical health is exercise. Maintaining a steady workout schedule is helpful, but even taking 5-minute study breaks to walk can help get your blood pumping faster and clear your head. Exercise also releases endorphins, which contribute to a positive feeling and can help combat test anxiety.

When you nurture your physical health, you are also contributing to your mental health. If your body is healthy, your mind is much more likely to be healthy as well. So take time to rest, nourish your body with healthy food and water, and get moving as much as possible. Taking these physical steps will make you stronger and more able to take the mental steps necessary to overcome test anxiety.

> **Review Video:** How to Stay Healthy and Prevent Test Anxiety
> Visit mometrix.com/academy and enter code: 877894

Mental Steps for Beating Test Anxiety

Working on the mental side of test anxiety can be more challenging, but as with the physical side, there are clear steps you can take to overcome it. As mentioned earlier, test anxiety often stems from lack of preparation, so the obvious solution is to prepare for the test. Effective studying may be the most important weapon you have for beating test anxiety, but you can and should employ several other mental tools to combat fear.

First, boost your confidence by reminding yourself of past success—tests or projects that you aced. If you're putting as much effort into preparing for this test as you did for those, there's no reason you should expect to fail here. Work hard to prepare; then trust your preparation.

Second, surround yourself with encouraging people. It can be helpful to find a study group, but be sure that the people you're around will encourage a positive attitude. If you spend time with others who are anxious or cynical, this will only contribute to your own anxiety. Look for others who are motivated to study hard from a desire to succeed, not from a fear of failure.

Third, reward yourself. A test is physically and mentally tiring, even without anxiety, and it can be helpful to have something to look forward to. Plan an activity following the test, regardless of the outcome, such as going to a movie or getting ice cream.

When you are taking the test, if you find yourself beginning to feel anxious, remind yourself that you know the material. Visualize successfully completing the test. Then take a few deep, relaxing breaths and return to it. Work through the questions carefully but with confidence, knowing that you are capable of succeeding.

Developing a healthy mental approach to test taking will also aid in other areas of life. Test anxiety affects more than just the actual test—it can be damaging to your mental health and even contribute to depression. It's important to beat test anxiety before it becomes a problem for more than testing.

Review Video: **Test Anxiety and Depression**
Visit mometrix.com/academy and enter code: 904704

Study Strategy

Being prepared for the test is necessary to combat anxiety, but what does being prepared look like? You may study for hours on end and still not feel prepared. What you need is a strategy for test prep. The next few pages outline our recommended steps to help you plan out and conquer the challenge of preparation.

Step 1: Scope Out the Test

Learn everything you can about the format (multiple choice, essay, etc.) and what will be on the test. Gather any study materials, course outlines, or sample exams that may be available. Not only will this help you to prepare, but knowing what to expect can help to alleviate test anxiety.

Step 2: Map Out the Material

Look through the textbook or study guide and make note of how many chapters or sections it has. Then divide these over the time you have. For example, if a book has 15 chapters and you have five days to study, you need to cover three chapters each day. Even better, if you have the time, leave an extra day at the end for overall review after you have gone through the material in depth.

If time is limited, you may need to prioritize the material. Look through it and make note of which sections you think you already have a good grasp on, and which need review. While you are studying, skim quickly through the familiar sections and take more time on the challenging parts. Write out your plan so you don't get lost as you go. Having a written plan also helps you feel more in control of the study, so anxiety is less likely to arise from feeling overwhelmed at the amount to cover.

Step 3: Gather Your Tools

Decide what study method works best for you. Do you prefer to highlight in the book as you study and then go back over the highlighted portions? Or do you type out notes of the important information? Or is it helpful to make flashcards that you can carry with you? Assemble the pens, index cards, highlighters, post-it notes, and any other materials you may need so you won't be distracted by getting up to find things while you study.

If you're having a hard time retaining the information or organizing your notes, experiment with different methods. For example, try color-coding by subject with colored pens, highlighters, or post-it notes. If you learn better by hearing, try recording yourself reading your notes so you can listen while in the car, working out, or simply sitting at your desk. Ask a friend to quiz you from your flashcards, or try teaching someone the material to solidify it in your mind.

Step 4: Create Your Environment

It's important to avoid distractions while you study. This includes both the obvious distractions like visitors and the subtle distractions like an uncomfortable chair (or a too-comfortable couch that makes you want to fall asleep). Set up the best study environment possible: good lighting and a comfortable work area. If background music helps you focus, you may want to turn it on, but otherwise keep the room quiet. If you are using a computer to take notes, be sure you don't have any other windows open, especially applications like social media, games, or anything else that could distract you. Silence your phone and turn off notifications. Be sure to keep water close by so you stay hydrated while you study (but avoid unhealthy drinks and snacks).

Also, take into account the best time of day to study. Are you freshest first thing in the morning? Try to set aside some time then to work through the material. Is your mind clearer in the afternoon or evening? Schedule your study session then. Another method is to study at the same time of day that you will take the test, so that your brain gets used to working on the material at that time and will be ready to focus at test time.

Step 5: Study!

Once you have done all the study preparation, it's time to settle into the actual studying. Sit down, take a few moments to settle your mind so you can focus, and begin to follow your study plan. Don't give in to distractions or let yourself procrastinate. This is your time to prepare so you'll be ready to fearlessly approach the test. Make the most of the time and stay focused.

Of course, you don't want to burn out. If you study too long you may find that you're not retaining the information very well. Take regular study breaks. For example, taking five minutes out of every hour to walk briskly, breathing deeply and swinging your arms, can help your mind stay fresh.

As you get to the end of each chapter or section, it's a good idea to do a quick review. Remind yourself of what you learned and work on any difficult parts. When you feel that you've mastered the material, move on to the next part. At the end of your study session, briefly skim through your notes again.

But while review is helpful, cramming last minute is NOT. If at all possible, work ahead so that you won't need to fit all your study into the last day. Cramming overloads your brain with more information than it can process and retain, and your tired mind may struggle to recall even previously learned information when it is overwhelmed with last-minute study. Also, the urgent nature of cramming and the stress placed on your brain contribute to anxiety. You'll be more likely to go to the test feeling unprepared and having trouble thinking clearly.

So don't cram, and don't stay up late before the test, even just to review your notes at a leisurely pace. Your brain needs rest more than it needs to go over the information again. In fact, plan to finish your studies by noon or early afternoon the day before the test. Give your brain the rest of the day to relax or focus on other things, and get a good night's sleep. Then you will be fresh for the test and better able to recall what you've studied.

Step 6: Take a practice test

Many courses offer sample tests, either online or in the study materials. This is an excellent resource to check whether you have mastered the material, as well as to prepare for the test format and environment.

Check the test format ahead of time: the number of questions, the type (multiple choice, free response, etc.), and the time limit. Then create a plan for working through them. For example, if you have 30 minutes to take a 60-question test, your limit is 30 seconds per question. Spend less time on the questions you know well so that you can take more time on the difficult ones.

If you have time to take several practice tests, take the first one open book, with no time limit. Work through the questions at your own pace and make sure you fully understand them. Gradually work up to taking a test under test conditions: sit at a desk with all study materials put away and set a timer. Pace yourself to make sure you finish the test with time to spare and go back to check your answers if you have time.

After each test, check your answers. On the questions you missed, be sure you understand why you missed them. Did you misread the question (tests can use tricky wording)? Did you forget the information? Or was it something you hadn't learned? Go back and study any shaky areas that the practice tests reveal.

Taking these tests not only helps with your grade, but also aids in combating test anxiety. If you're already used to the test conditions, you're less likely to worry about it, and working through tests until you're scoring well gives you a confidence boost. Go through the practice tests until you feel comfortable, and then you can go into the test knowing that you're ready for it.

Test Tips

On test day, you should be confident, knowing that you've prepared well and are ready to answer the questions. But aside from preparation, there are several test day strategies you can employ to maximize your performance.

First, as stated before, get a good night's sleep the night before the test (and for several nights before that, if possible). Go into the test with a fresh, alert mind rather than staying up late to study.

Try not to change too much about your normal routine on the day of the test. It's important to eat a nutritious breakfast, but if you normally don't eat breakfast at all, consider eating just a protein bar. If you're a coffee drinker, go ahead and have your normal coffee. Just make sure you time it so that the caffeine doesn't wear off right in the middle of your test. Avoid sugary beverages, and drink enough water to stay hydrated but not so much that you need a restroom break 10 minutes into the test. If your test isn't first thing in the morning, consider going for a walk or doing a light workout before the test to get your blood flowing.

Allow yourself enough time to get ready, and leave for the test with plenty of time to spare so you won't have the anxiety of scrambling to arrive in time. Another reason to be early is to select a good seat. It's helpful to sit away from doors and windows, which can be distracting. Find a good seat, get out your supplies, and settle your mind before the test begins.

When the test begins, start by going over the instructions carefully, even if you already know what to expect. Make sure you avoid any careless mistakes by following the directions.

Then begin working through the questions, pacing yourself as you've practiced. If you're not sure on an answer, don't spend too much time on it, and don't let it shake your confidence. Either skip it and come back later, or eliminate as many wrong answers as possible and guess among the remaining ones. Don't dwell on these questions as you continue—put them out of your mind and focus on what lies ahead.

Be sure to read all of the answer choices, even if you're sure the first one is the right answer. Sometimes you'll find a better one if you keep reading. But don't second-guess yourself if you do immediately know the answer. Your gut instinct is usually right. Don't let test anxiety rob you of the information you know.

If you have time at the end of the test (and if the test format allows), go back and review your answers. Be cautious about changing any, since your first instinct tends to be correct, but make sure you didn't misread any of the questions or accidentally mark the wrong answer choice. Look over any you skipped and make an educated guess.

At the end, leave the test feeling confident. You've done your best, so don't waste time worrying about your performance or wishing you could change anything. Instead, celebrate the successful completion of this test. And finally, use this test to learn how to deal with anxiety even better next time.

> **Review Video:** 5 Tips to Beat Test Anxiety
> Visit mometrix.com/academy and enter code: 570656

Important Qualification

Not all anxiety is created equal. If your test anxiety is causing major issues in your life beyond the classroom or testing center, or if you are experiencing troubling physical symptoms related to your anxiety, it may be a sign of a serious physiological or psychological condition. If this sounds like your situation, we strongly encourage you to seek professional help.

Thank You

We at Mometrix would like to extend our heartfelt thanks to you, our friend and patron, for allowing us to play a part in your journey. It is a privilege to serve people from all walks of life who are unified in their commitment to building the best future they can for themselves.

The preparation you devote to these important testing milestones may be the most valuable educational opportunity you have for making a real difference in your life. We encourage you to put your heart into it—that feeling of succeeding, overcoming, and yes, conquering will be well worth the hours you've invested.

We want to hear your story, your struggles and your successes, and if you see any opportunities for us to improve our materials so we can help others even more effectively in the future, please share that with us as well. **The team at Mometrix would be absolutely thrilled to hear from you!** So please, send us an email (support@mometrix.com) and let's stay in touch.

If you'd like some additional help, check out these other resources we offer for your exam:

http://MometrixFlashcards.com/CaliforniaStandardsTests